PENGUIN BOOKS

PARENTS ARE PEOPLE TOO

Katherine Gordy Levine is a parent. She is a professor of social work at Columbia University School of
Social Work, where she teaches adolescent development, and is the author of *When Good Kids Do Bad
Things*. In addition to heading her own consulting
business, Emotional Fitness Training®, Inc., she also
directs a crisis service for the Visiting Nurse Service
of New York, teaching parenting skills and feeling
management to families in their homes. For thirteen
years she and her husband were special-need foster
parents. She lives in Harrison, New York.

PARENTS ARE
PEOPLE TOO

An Emotional
Fitness Program
for Parents

KATHERINE GORDY LEVINE

PENGUIN BOOKS

PENGUIN BOOKS

Published by the Penguin Group
Penguin Books USA Inc., 375 Hudson Street,
New York, New York 10014, U.S.A.
Penguin Books Ltd, 27 Wrights Lane, London W8 5TZ, England
Penguin Books Australia Ltd, Ringwood, Victoria, Australia
Penguin Books Canada Ltd, 10 Alcorn Avenue,
Toronto, Ontario, Canada M4V 3B2
Penguin Books (N.Z.) Ltd, 182–190 Wairau Road,
Auckland 10, New Zealand

Penguin Books Ltd, Registered Offices: Harmondsworth, Middlesex, England

First published in Penguin Books 1997

10 9 8 7 6 5 4 3 2 1

A Note to the Reader
The individuals described in this book are composites of more than one
real person. The actions and statements ascribed to each individual is
a combination of the actions and statements of the persons on
whom that characterization is based.

LIBRARY OF CONGRESS CATALOGING IN PUBLICATION DATA

Levine, Katherine Gordy.
    Parents are people too: an emotional fitness program for parents/
Katherine Gordy Levine.
        p.   cm.
    ISBN 0 14 02.3619 8 (pbk.)
    1. Parents—Attitudes.   2. Parenting—Psychological aspects.
3. Self-control.   4. Emotions.   I. Title.
HQ755.83.L49   1997
155.6'46—dc21   96-39204

Printed in the United States of America
Set in Minion
Designed by Claudyne Bianco Bedell

*This book is dedicated to all
parents and all children.
If we are only for our own
children, we fail all children.*

PREFACE

Why
I Wrote
This Book

As foster parents for thirteen years, my husband, David, and I cared for a constantly changing group of children and adolescents. Sometimes two, sometimes four, occasionally six or seven children lived with us as members of our family. By the time we stopped, we had served as foster parents to a total of 369 kids.

Every one of them taught us something. But one of the most important lessons was realizing that when I handled my feelings properly, I handled the kids better. If I felt guilty or angry or anxious and let those feelings control me, the kids and I suffered.

PREFACE

I never found a book devoted to helping me handle my feelings so I could be a better parent. Even though my children are now grown, I have yet to see a book for parents that deals specifically with this aspect of parenting. I decided, therefore, to write this book.

My intent is to help you stay in charge of the negative feelings that accompany raising a child. The book will teach you specific skills including feeling awareness, self-soothing, distracting, focusing on what is important, disputing, giving feedback, proper expression of feelings, acceptance, and radical acceptance. These skills form my Emotional Fitness Training® program for parents. Learning and practicing these skills will help you stay in charge of your feelings. When you are in charge of your feelings, you will feel better and will find life as a parent easier and more enjoyable. This is my promise for the book and my hope for all parents.

Katherine Gordy Levine

ACKNOWLEDGMENTS

Just as it takes a village to raise a child, so it takes many to create a book. I want to acknowledge all who have helped this book come to be. First, I was a child and a sister and a student. My parents, my brothers, my friends, the many other mentors and teachers who contributed to my move from babe-in-arms to adult had a part in this book.

In time I met David. I once read a love poem that praised a lover for helping his beloved become all she could be. That requires a rare generosity. Without David's generosity of spirit and faith in me, this book would not have been.

ACKNOWLEDGMENTS

Nor could it have come to be without my having experienced the slings and arrows as well as the joys and pleasures of parenthood. My two sons taught me much about the importance of learning to control my feelings if I was to nurture theirs. I am so glad I have been able to be part of their lives. The other children in my life—my former foster children, my nieces, my nephews, my cousins, my friends' children, my clients, my students have underscored the lessons my sons taught. Each is part of this book.

And then there have been all the parents I have known. They are too numerous to name. Some live in the poverty of Mott Haven, others in million-dollar mansions. Most live in between these two material states. Some have been clients, some friends, some passing acquaintances. All taught me something of value. Their strength, hope, and experiences are part of this book.

And finally there are those who earn their living as part of the publishing world. The connection between my dreams and my hopes for this book began with Roberta Markel, who graced one of my classrooms for a semester. She thought I had some things of value to say and introduced me to her husband, Bob Markel. Bob ultimately became my agent and his faith in this book has been an important factor in its creation. Then there are the people at Viking Penguin—Mindy Werner, Susan Hans O'Connor, and Cathy Dexter—who stood by me as the book went through its many transformations. My strength as a writer lies in my willingness to rewrite. Mindy, Susan, and Cathy's strengths lie in their ability to separate the good from the not so good and to make the good better.

ACKNOWLEDGMENTS

I thank them for their patience and their hard work. This is their book as much as it is mine.

Finally, this book comes through me because of the grace granted me by my Higher Power—the force outside me that has graciously allowed me to be of service in some small way to the children and parents I have been lucky enough to touch. I have been blessed more than most and I am grateful.

CONTENTS

PARENTS ARE
PEOPLE TOO

1

Your
Feelings
Come First

No matter what your child's age or stage, your feelings must come first, for you cannot take care of a child's feelings unless you first take care of your own. You don't believe me? See if any of these bits of conversation sound familiar:

> "I can't stand her whining; it drives me crazy."

> "You aren't supposed to give in to temper tantrums, but his go on for so long, I can't take it."

"He didn't come in until 2 A.M. I was so frightened I couldn't sleep. And when he walked through the door, I yelled for a half hour straight. When I was done yelling, he told me the car had broken down and he'd walked eight miles to get home. Too damn proud to knock on someone's door and call for help."

Children scare, anger, and hurt parents, and when parents don't handle their fear, anger, or hurt properly, children suffer; hurt accumulates and negative exchanges mount. Often the ties that bind become strained and sometimes severed. Avoiding this stress and strain takes many emotional fitness skills. Most parents have *some* of the requisite skills; this book teaches additional skills and helps you improve those you already possess. Everyone can learn to take better care of their feelings so that neither children nor parents suffer unnecessarily.

How? By reading and practicing the exercises in this book. Whether you have one child or a dozen, whether your child is still demanding 2 A.M. feedings or is out with the family car until then, you need to be in charge of your feelings. This book will show you how.

OUR FEELINGS CAN BURN OUR CHILDREN (AND VICE VERSA)

Being a parent is tough. Bad follows good. Good follows bad. And you never know when one will replace the other. The bad is rarely in your power to predict, and often not in your power to change. One thing is predictable, though: by the time a child makes it through the early years and into the teens, most parents identify at one time or another with this African proverb:

> A cow gave birth to a fire. She wanted to lick it, but it burned her. She wanted to leave it, but it was her child.

Sometimes life burns our children. Sometimes our children burn us. Life with our children can be so searing we want to leave them. But they are our children; we cannot leave them. So we fuss and fume and rage over them. We endure the bad times and wait for the good times, for when the pain dies down, we delight in our children. They are our hope, our joy, our wonder of wonders.

No matter what age your child, your feelings are intertwined with the things your child feels, says, and does. No one can stir your good feelings the way your child can. No one can stir your negative feelings the way your child can. Sometimes the negative feelings are created by your child. Sometimes they start with you. But whether they start with your child or with you, *you* are the one who must stay in control. You are the parent.

When we are lucky and when we work hard, the balance of pain and joy can be tipped in our favor; we can do more than endure the bad times. We can master the bad and survive the pain our children inflict without losing our love. We must, however, work at this throughout all our children's growing-up years, for often, when we gain control of our feelings in one situation, a new situation develops in which our child often socks it to us. Some examples:

- Your baby smiles and joy fills your entire being. The same baby cries all night three nights in a row and you come to know despair, powerlessness, and rage.

- Your two-year-old finally sheds her diaper; you applaud with glee. Three days later the same child has an "accident" on your mother-in-law's brand-new, bone-white rug. Shame and anger invade your heart.

- Your seven-year-old masters riding a two-wheeler and you share the thrill of victory. The next morning he rides the same bike off to see a friend and anxiety haunts your every move until he is safely home.

- Your teenager stays out all night and you die a thousand deaths. She comes home trailing stardust in her hair and tells you she fell asleep under the stars at an outdoor concert. She was with a boy you want to vaporize. Rage consumes you.

- Your high school graduate drives you crazy the month before he heads off to college. You can't believe his obnoxiousness. You can't

believe how happy you are when he leaves.
You also can't believe how empty the house
is the next day, and how much you miss him.

Even infants can be harmed when parental feelings slip
out of control. It happens more than we like to admit; I
lost control with one of my sons when he was just a two-
month-old infant. I did not hurt him either physically or
emotionally, but I was a heartbeat away from shaking
him violently.

This son had an ear infection. David, my husband,
was away and I was home alone with the baby, who spent
most of his time crying unless he was being walked. So
I spent the night walking, and the longer I walked, the
more I felt I was being tortured.

Finally, as the sun was rising, the baby fell into a
deep sleep. I put him down. I don't remember collapsing
into my bed, but he and I were still sleeping when the
doorbell started ringing at about 9:30 A.M. I raced to the
door, scared the ringing would wake the baby. It did, for
as I opened the door, he started shrieking again. The
Electrolux salesman barely escaped with his life. I dragged
myself back to the baby's room and picked him up and
started walking the floor again. Only now he wouldn't
stop crying.

I snapped in fifteen minutes. How? I put the baby
in the middle of our bed and stood over him yelling. He
stopped crying for a minute, gave me a long look, and
then resumed his shrieking. At that point, I punctuated
my yells by pounding on the bed at his feet. I was as

frantic as he was. I wanted to pick him up and shake him hard.

Fortunately, Brutus, our dog, rushed into the room. Brutus was a boxer by breed and a pacifist by disposition. His mission in life was to stop any fight in his vicinity. On the day I flipped out, my yelling alerted him to trouble brewing. Once in the room, he understood immediately what had to be done. He pushed between baby, bed, and me. When I yelled at him, he growled back and kept pushing me away from the bed. He ultimately pushed me out the door.

Good Brutus. He was right; I couldn't go on. I called a friend who came and took over. She sent me to bed, and when I woke up twelve hours later David was home and the baby's ear infection had cleared up. Nevertheless, "Sheriff" Brutus kept a watchful eye on me for several days. Every time I was with the baby, he was there too. He worried about me and I didn't blame him. I had lost control. That fact, however, did not make me a bad parent. It made me a parent who let stress build to the danger point.

LEARNING TO MANAGE FEELINGS—THE FIRST STEPS

Few parents who spend time caring for and disciplining their child stay in control all the time. Losing control is not good, but all parents have a snapping point, and that is why all parents need to learn to manage feelings. The more you know about managing your feelings, the less likely you are to snap in ways that are permanently damaging to your child.

Some feelings are come-and-go feelings. Like the ripples from a rock thrown into a quiet pond, the feelings spread and fade, and quiet is restored until someone throws another "rock." These feelings are best lived through and then ignored. To live through some of these feelings, you need calming and self-soothing skills.

Other feelings are like dangerous currents; if ignored, they sweep you away. These feelings need first to be ridden out. Fight a riptide and it will pull you out to sea, calming and self-soothing skills will help you ride a dangerous feeling to its end.

Few feelings require immediate action. Too many people, however, act on strong feelings as if confronting a fire. Too often, the fire exists only in the person's imagination. Moreover, even if confronted with a blazing fire ready to consume you and your child, you have to pause for a half a second to decide the fastest route out of the house. Which brings us to the golden rule of feeling management: *Think before acting.*

In order to think before you act, you need to learn how to calm down when negative feelings run high, and you need to know how to decide what needs acting on. Both are emotional fitness skills. The major emotional fitness skills involve:

1. recognizing the start of a feeling

2. measuring the growth of feelings

3. calming the body when a feeling threatens to overwhelm

4. changing the flow of negative feelings when that is possible

5. deciding what needs acting on

6. accepting and living with negative feelings when changing them is not possible.

These skills come as easily as sitting up to a lucky few. If you aren't among those few, however, don't be discouraged; this book is here to help you.

HOW THIS BOOK WORKS

The exercises in this book are part of an Emotional Fitness Training® program for parents. I developed this program as one of a number of programs forming the foundation of my consulting and training company, Emotional Fitness Training, Inc. Like sit-ups, each exercise has been created from things we do naturally.

The exercises may take time to learn, but, once learned, most can be practiced easily and in less than a minute. Once you have learned the exercises, practice four or five times a day regularly for at least two weeks. Yes, this sounds like a lot, but practicing the exercises takes only five or ten minutes a day. Practicing in the order suggested works best, as each exercise builds on the previous one.

Let's try one—Counting Your Breath. Learning to count your breath calms your body and is part of the skill of self-soothing. Self-soothing helps you calm down and think about what is happening and what to do. Even when danger threatens, you should try to take a breath so you can focus your thoughts. Self-soothing helps you combat the painful aspects of negative feelings.

Counting Your Breath is a fairly common meditation exercise. I can hear some of you saying, "Oh no, those things just never work for me." They didn't use to work for me either. We are not all the same. What works for one, doesn't for another. I have designed my exercises with this in mind.

Here's how to do my first Emotional Fitness Training exercise.

Counting Your Breath
Shift your focus from reading to observing how you are sitting or reclining. Notice the position of your body. Shift your body into a comfortable position. Notice how it feels to shift and move and settle into a more comfortable position. When you have found a comfortable position, take a deep, calming breath by breathing in deeply through your nose as you slowly count to four, holding your breath for another slow count of four, and finally breathing out to a slow count of four. (As you breathe in, think the word "and." As you breathe out, think the number one. As you breathe in again, think the

word "and" again; as you breathe out, think the next number.)

Some like to close their eyes at this point, while others like to focus on a spot directly in front of their eyes or on the ceiling. Try shutting your eyes. Observe what happens. Then try focusing on some spot in front of you. Trying looking at the ceiling. Observe the difference. Stay with whichever feels most comfortable and concentrate on what it feels like to breathe in and to breathe out. Notice the air in your nostrils as you breathe in. Is it cool or warm? Where does that air go? How does it feel to breathe out? Now just breathe and count each breath. Count five breaths.

If a thought intrudes, notice it as passively as possible and go back to observing your breath. If you forget or lose track of your counting, start again at one. When you have reached the count of five, smile a gentle smile —not a grin, just a gentle Mona Lisa or Buddha smile. Repeat the entire exercise one more time. When you are done, end with the smile, stretch, and go on.

Once learned, every exercise in this book is as easy to do as Counting Your Breath. They're somewhat easier than sit-ups, but, as with sit-ups, the results are not instantly apparent. However, the more you do, the better the results. Give each of the exercises in this book a fair try and remember that practice is part of making the exercises work. Trying such an exercise once in a workshop or a class or when reading a book is not a fair test. You wouldn't expect to tighten your abdominal muscles by doing two or three sit-ups. You can't expect to improve a tennis stroke in a few minutes of practicing. In order to work, the exercises in this book need to be practiced diligently.

FINDING TIME TO PRACTICE IS IMPORTANT

It's sad to say, but many of you will be hard-pressed to find ten minutes a day to practice these exercises. If you can't figure out how to find time to practice, try doing the exercises any time you have a spare minute. If you don't think you have any spare minutes, use waste time. Waste time includes standing in a line, riding a bus, subway, or taxi, sitting in traffic, or anytime and anywhere you have to wait for something or someone. The more you practice, the more skilled you will become at managing your feelings. Your life will improve and your child's life will improve. I know—mine did. As I developed and practiced these exercises, my ability to cope with negative feelings improved, and that improved my life. Before I teach you more exercises, however, you need to learn more about feelings in general and about your feelings specifically.

2

How
Feelings
Begin

Knowing what starts a feeling is a major feeling management skill. You need to be aware of your feelings if you are going to take charge of them. This means you need to know how feelings start.

All feelings start in bodily arousals. For example, a baby's crying is designed to make parents sit up and take note. It is an arousing event. When our children were babies, David and I often had the following conversation:

"The baby's been crying for hours. It is driving me crazy."

"He's only been crying for ten minutes. You just have to ignore it. You are too sensitive."

"It's hard enough dealing with his crying without you getting on my case."

"For Pete's sake, calm down. I'm not on your case. I'm trying to help."

"Remind me why we married!"

Does a baby's crying drive you crazy, or can you stay calm and unaffected? Do you and your child's other parent quarrel about how to handle the crying? When a baby cries, some very specific things happen to the grown-ups in the vicinity. Their skin contracts, their blood pressure rises. These are strong arousals and they make most people feel edgy, and vastly relieved when the crying stops. The unpleasantness is nature's way of guaranteeing that crying babies will be picked up, fed, and comforted.

All feelings begin when something arouses your interest. Some arousals are caused by external events, things that happen outside our body. These include a crying baby, thunder and lightning, scary news programs, loud noises, and the hurtful or happy words of other people. Physiological arousals, like being tired or hungry, are sources of arousal from inside our body that occur because of our body's physical state. Thoughts (caused by both internal and external events) also arouse. Understanding each of these arousals is the key to understanding the start of feelings.

CHANGES IN THE BODY'S PHYSIOLOGICAL STATE START FEELINGS

Hold your breath as long as you can. The longer you hold your breath, the more pressure you will feel to let it go and draw in more air. Holding your breath leads to a change in your body's chemical state. Normally, little emotion is associated with taking a breath. If you couldn't take a breath, however, the physiological changes would eventually end up in a feeling commonly called fear. If someone were keeping you from breathing, the arousal might become anger instead of fear. But both would begin with the same physiological arousal.

Arousals are the body's physiological response to something outside or inside of us. Step one in a feeling chain is always arousal—some sort of change in our body's chemical state. Step two is when a name is attached to the arousal, but the arousal begins the feeling. As Jerome Kagan, psychiatrist and Harvard researcher, in his book *The Nature of the Child*, notes:

> Although scientists do not agree on all of the events that participate in an emotion (some scientists place the origin of emotion in the brain, while others locate it in changes in the facial

muscles), all agree that some change in internal state is a necessary feature of the phenomena called emotional.

But sometimes what arouses us is only or mostly related to a physical need. So the first step in deciding if the arousal is being caused mainly by a physical or an emotional state is to know about the physiologically based changes and arousal. These include:

Biological clock difficulties such as jet lag.

Hunger—dieting, skipping meals.

Hormonal shifts (adolescence, pregnancy, premenstrual tension, unmet sexual needs).

Illness.

Physical injury.

Chronic pain.

Sleep deprivation or general fatigue.

Chemicals ingested or injected into the body—medication, alcohol, other drugs.

One mother came to my office confused and upset, because for the first twenty-five days in her menstrual cycle she is all her child could ask for—loving, attentive, calm, serene, patient. Then, as she put it: "I become the wicked witch from Hansel and Gretel for three days. Finally, I start to cry and I can't stop for an hour or so. When I have finally cried enough, I can get back to being a good mother again."

Yes, this mother had premenstrual syndrome (PMS), and it played havoc with her emotions and her children. Some detective work ferreted out the hormonal nature of her rages. Once properly identified, the onset of symptoms became recognizable as advance warnings.

Mom and I developed an early warning system for the family: A "danger day" sign went up on the refrigerator at the onset of her Broomstick days. The sign told her family to tread more lightly or suffer the consequences. Confused signals were clarified. Of course, in an ideal family, this would mean Mom would get lots of tender loving care during those days. This is not likely to happen in most families. You settle for what you can get in today's busy world.

A father who also was given to periodic bouts of anger couldn't map his as regularly as PMS Mom, but a little detective work revealed that his outbursts occurred whenever his normal exercise routine was disrupted. He suffered from what I call Exercise Interruptus Syndrome (EIS). Exercising releases tensions and feel-good hormones. Not getting his exercise made this dad irritable and prone to anger. He learned to post a "Didn't Exercise Today" sign to warn his family and to motivate him either to get to work on exercising or controlling his negative feelings.

Accumulated sexual tension also can set up an arousal chain. This is often an unrecognized arousal. Most likely to be missed or to set up a feeling chain are sexual tensions related to an unacceptable arousal. I nickname these unacceptable sexual arousals USA tensions. They involve getting turned on when you don't think you should. For example, when I was a teenager, I couldn't understand why my father got angry whenever he saw teenagers necking in public. He'd grumble and complain and talk under his breath. It was one of his less loveable quirks. I didn't understand at the time, but I now realize this quirk was probably a case of USA. I saw the light when one of our first foster children sat in our living room and necked with her boyfriend. I couldn't believe how annoyed I got. "Just like Dad," I thought.

So why the anger? Why not just enjoy the sexy feelings? Because being turned on by my necking foster children was unacceptable. A grown woman is not supposed to get turned on watching two kids neck. So I turned the arousal to anger. I assume the same thing had happened to dear not-so-old Dad.

PSYCHOLOGICAL FACTORS INTENSIFY PHYSIOLOGICALLY BASED AROUSALS

Feelings may start in a physical arousal, but psychological factors come into play very quickly. Once we are aroused, the brain begins to evaluate the arousal. The brain has to decide what the arousal means, whether it is good or bad, and what can or should be done. Often this intensifies the arousal and strengthens the feeling. This is what happened to Dad and me watching teenagers neck.

Other physiological arousals can start a feeling chain that ends far afield from its original starting point. You need to pay attention to such situations. Dieting? Keep an extra hold on your temper. Postmenstrual? Wear a red hat—warn the world to take care. Sleepless? Go as slowly as possible the next day. Learning to spot and then deal with physiologically based arousals is an important skill when it comes to taking charge of your feelings. Here's how:

How to Handle Physiologically Based Arousals

1. Stay in touch with the various physiological states of your body and its fluctuating needs.

2. Meet those needs as consistently and regularly as possible.

3. When physical fitness is not at its best, let others know you are under more stress than usual and that tangling with you is probably not the wisest choice to make.

4. Expect less of yourself; do less.

5. Expect less of others.

6. Give yourself lots of tender loving care, but don't give in to temper tantrums—yours or another's.

EXTERNAL EVENTS AROUSE

As already mentioned, some arousals are caused by external events. Something outside of your body causes you to take notice. Most often external sources of arousal involve other people: Your child slips and seems to be headed for a painful fall; your heart lurches, your brain splits, your stomach sinks. Asked what you are feeling at that moment, you would probably respond, "Fear." Your child doesn't fall, you let out a sigh, your muscles relax. You feel relief.

Your fear and your relief were caused by external events. In addition to serving as a signal, arousal motivates and readies the body to take action. Maybe as your child was teetering on the brink of a fall, you leapt from your seat and started toward her. Adrenaline was pumping into your bloodstream along with lots of other chemicals. When action wasn't needed, your fear subsided and your body relaxed.

Half-Held Breaths Heighten Arousal

You know if you see your child teetering on the edge of a flight of stairs and you can't reach her in time to help her regain her balance, you "hold your breath" while you wait to see what is going to happen. When you have twenty things to do that each take a minute to do, but you only have ten minutes to do them all, you are probably not breathing fully and deeply. Or if your child interrupts you as you are about to leave the house for an important meeting, you probably half-hold your breath while listening to what your child has to say.

When you half-hold your breath, your body feels the same sort of tightness it feels when you hold your breath on purpose. Whether or not the bodily sensations will be called "fear," "anxiety," "curiosity," "hope," or any other number of feelings will depend on how you ultimately come to explain the arousal. Whatever the ultimate name, the arousal always comes first. Because half-held breaths increase arousal and because a major skill in learning to manage feelings involves learning to quiet arousals, let's learn another Emotional Fitness Training exercise.

This exercise involves learning to breathe slowly and fully from your abdomen (diaphragmatic breathing is the official name for this type of breathing). Breathing from your diaphragm most of the time also adds to the effectiveness of the Counting Your Breath exercise (see pages 9–10).

Breathing from Your Abdomen

Take a minute to observe how you breathe. Breathe only through your nose; breathing through your mouth can start a pattern of gulping air that interferes with calm abdominal breathing. So does consciously taking deep breaths one after the other. Some people teach you to breathe deeply in an effort to calm arousal, but the studies all show that can be counterproductive. Calming breaths are slow, natural abdominal breaths. Some will be deep, others not so deep.

Count your breath for a minute. Remember how?

Take a cleansing breath; then count every time you breathe out. When you reach the fifth breath, smile. After several breaths, try to figure out if you breathe more from your chest or more from your abdomen.

Observe how you breathe. Put one hand on your chest near your breastbone and the other on your tummy between your belly button and your pubic bone. Breathe normally. As you breathe, notice which hand moves first as you breathe in. The hand on your chest? That is thoracic or chest breathing, which is good to use when you need to rev yourself up for a moment or two, but not so useful when you need to calm down. If the hand on your belly is the one that moves, you are breathing through your diaphragm, which is more calming than chest breathing.

Generally, we breathe more naturally in one of these two modes. A baby breathes most of the time from the abdomen and only every so often takes a chest breath. As we grow up, however, we begin to hold our stomach in, and that often means we are not breathing in an easy, relaxed way that helps us stay calm.

Still not certain how you are breathing? Here's another way to tell. Take a deep breath in and, as you do so, suck your stomach in. Hold it in as you breathe out. Next time, consciously relax your stomach and, as you breathe in, imagine a balloon in your stomach filling with air. Try also to make a conscious effort to push your stomach out. When you breathe out, imagine the same balloon collapsing and then make a conscious effort to tighten your stomach. Still not certain? It might help to lie down on your back and place a book on your abdomen; then make the book move as you breathe in. Or press your hands slightly down on your abdomen and push against them.

Feeling silly that you can't tell how you breathe? Don't. I took almost three weeks to figure out the difference. Then it took another three weeks to become comfortable shifting from one form of breathing to the other. Taking the time was worth the effort; learning to breathe from my diaphragm did help me stay calm.

Here is another suggestion that will help you shift when you notice you are breathing from your chest. For the next two breaths, breathe in normally, but as you are breathing out, extend your exhaling for a longer than usual period of time. Notice how it feels to really empty out your lungs. If you breathe out long enough your lungs will empty and a small vacuum will be created so that when you breathe in, it will be a long, deep, abdominal breath.

Once you have learned to breathe abdominally, you will find you are able to switch easily from one mode of breathing to another. Don't feel you have to take every breath abdominally; try to make every four out of five breaths an abdominal breath.

Practice learning to control how you breathe until you can consciously switch from chest to diaphragm breathing at will. Breathing is something you have to do anyway, and learning to breathe properly will make breathing work for you, not against you. Remember, half-held breaths interfere with staying calm. This is one exercise where finding time to practice is no further than a breath away.

Once you learn how to breathe from your diaphragm or chest at will, you can also use this ability to calm down or rev up various arousals at will. Remember, even in a dangerous situation you want to center before acting. Being centered means being alertly relaxed. A deep abdominal breath centers you quickly. Once you find that you can take one deep abdominal breath and center, start and end each emotional fitness exercise with a centering breath.

Not all external arousal sources are obvious. Sometimes what first arouses can be so subtle we might not even be consciously aware of what we are responding to. A look on another person's face or a barely discernable shift in someone's tone of voice can start a feeling chain just as surely as the sight of a child heading for a fall. A feeling chain started by either internal or external arousal sources get added to or strengthened by our thoughts.

THE ROLE OF THOUGHTS

Thinking about food can make you hungry, thinking about sex can make you feel sexy. Thoughts about yesterday's anger can make you angry again. Recalling fear can recreate fear. As an exercise in feeling awareness, let's re-create anger. I'll pick a memory from the time I was a foster parent:

It's three o'clock in the morning and the doorbell rings. The ringer leans on the bell, determined to awaken everyone. The ringer is Sarah, our foster daughter. She's been gone for two days. I crawl out of bed, silently cursing under my breath. Sarah is far from one of my favorite kids.

That's right. I am no Mother Teresa. Some kids are born very difficult to love; others develop unloving ways as they grow. Whatever the cause, the fact remains that only a saint could love some of our foster children, and I'm no saint.

Sarah was one of those kids. Nasty, loud, determined to get her own way and a disruptive influence on the other kids, Sarah was also cruel to our pets, to the other kids in the house, and even to the baby.

David and I had been hoping this time she'd "run away" long enough so we could officially take her off our rolls. That meant she had to be gone two full days. But Sarah was smart as well as nasty. Sarah liked living with us. When she ran, it wasn't away. It was to a party, to visit a boyfriend, to connect with old friends. Sarah also knew the rules: return within two days or another kid would be moved in to take your place and you'd be moved to another home. Sarah always returned in time to keep someone else from taking her place.

I would have liked to let Sarah cool her heels outside a bit longer, but the ringing of the bell was about to wake everyone else up. So I scurried downstairs as fast as I could, unlocked the door, and threw it open.

Sarah pushed past me and announced, "You took your time. I'm going to complain to my probation officer. You aren't supposed to lock me out."

This was par for Sarah. A legal beagle, she knew all the rules, and in a nonsecure detention home, which was our official designation, kids couldn't be locked out. I was angry but prepared; we'd been through this a number of times. Sarah would deliver some sort of little speech designed to anger and then head up to her room. Usually, I would say nothing.

This time, however, Sarah didn't head right up to her room. Instead, she turned, looked me up and down, and said, "God, that's an ugly robe. You look awful. I'm hungry. Make me some breakfast."

I turned my version of what David and I call the "killing stare" on Sarah and she decided not to press the point. She went up to her room, muttering obscenities under her breath. The nerve of her. Looking me up and down as though I were dirt and then commanding me to get her breakfast. And she was the one who was breaking all the rules, being rude and crude.

When I think about Sarah, not only can I re-create my anger, but my body responds as well. The muscles of my face set in an angry scowl. What does that feel like? My eyebrows pull together, my eyes narrow, my lips pull down and compress, my teeth clench, and my jaw tightens.

Thus past thoughts can latch on to current situations and add to their intensity without our conscious awareness. Several months after Sarah left our care, I remember finding myself unaccountably angry at another foster child. I finally realized this girl looked a little like Sarah. The anger I had felt toward Sarah was rearoused and inappropriately transferred to my new foster daughter—a current situation and relationship contaminated by past thoughts and feelings.

UNCERTAINTY LEADS TO FEELINGS

Uncertainty—not knowing what is happening or what to think—also starts feelings. According to the cognitive theorists—including George Kelly, Leon Festinger, and Jerome Kagan—a major source of arousal is uncertainty. (Benjamin Franklin would have agreed—he noted in his autobiography that uneasiness was the main reason people did much of what they did.) Whether called uneasiness or uncertainty, this source of arousal begins with the brain's efforts to make sense of the world. Making sense of things helps you take charge; when you know what is happening, you know what to do.

Remember the last time your child was irritable and cranky? You couldn't figure out what was bothering her. Then she began rubbing her ear. You realized she probably had an ear infection. While you weren't happy with the fact that your child was getting sick, you were relieved to know what was going on; not knowing created uncertainty.

Knowing did not resolve all your uncomfortable feelings, however. You started worrying about whether you had done something to cause the baby to get sick. Uncertainty. You worried about whether the baby's hearing would be affected. Uncertainty. You worried about whether you should call the doctor now or wait until the morning. Uncertainty. So many things to know, to decide, and to be sure about.

George Kelly, in his book *The Psychology of Personal Constructs*, stresses the importance of our need to make sense of our world:

Man looks at his world through transparent patterns, or templates, which he creates and then attempts to fit over the realities of which the world is composed. The fit is not always very good, yet without such patterns, the world appears to be such an undifferentiated homogeneity that man is unable to make any sense out of it. Even a poor fit is more helpful to him than nothing at all.

According to the cognitive theorists, once an object is sufficiently known to be stored in memory, it becomes a "reality." When something contradicts this reality, uncertainty arises. Baby puts together the idea of a face and for a while he assumes all faces are one. Then, at about six months, he becomes more astute. He realizes that not all faces are Mom's and Dad's. Stranger anxiety is born.

Kagan would name stranger anxiety fear or uncertainty created by the infant's ability to remember and compare faces. The familiar face is known and predictable; the stranger's face is unknown, unpredictable, and, therefore, frightening. Kagan and the other cognitive theorists believe most feelings start in one type of uncertainty or another. Kagan notes in *The Nature of the Child*:

After biological needs are cared for, children and adults seem to spend much of their time and energy in a narrow psychological space bounded on the right by boredom with the familiar and on the left by the terror of the bizarre.

Kagan also believes the most painful uncertainties are those related to what he calls psychological uncertainty involving other people. The most painful psychological uncertainty deals with whether others love and respect us, whether we are good people, whether we are competent, whether we are in control, and whether our core beliefs can stand challenges from life, opposing beliefs, and our own behavior. Raising a child creates uncertainty in each of these areas.

The Uncertainties Facing Parents

If you cannot comfort a crying baby, you might feel incompetent; you might feel powerless and out of control. If you get angry at a crying baby, faith in your sense of goodness gets shaken. You might question whether the crying means the baby won't love you. You might question whether you love the baby. Uncertainty piles upon uncertainty. Being a parent constantly creates uncertainty.

Remember the fear when you first brought your baby home from the hospital? Was he breathing? What did his crying mean? Was he really getting enough milk from breastfeeding? Had you failed him because you weren't breastfeeding? New situations are fraught with uncertainty and none more so than having a new baby.

When a baby starts walking, more uncertainty is created; newly walking babies can walk right into danger. Yet another uncertainty is created once a baby masters walking. Walking babies can defy, run from parents, and hide in small places parents can't get to. Walking, running babies can leave parents feeling powerless and out of control.

It doesn't get better either, for soon the baby starts talking and almost simultaneously learns to say no. The Terrible Twos set in, and the Terrible Twos mean colliding wills and new sources of uncertainty.

And, sooner or later, your dimpled darling says, "I hate you." You know this is anger talking, but, oh, the uncertainty it creates.

As your child grows, other questions and uncertainties mount. Is he too aggressive? Does he give in to others too easily? Is he too independent, too dependent? Uncertainty upon uncertainty.

Your child falls seriously ill or is seriously injured. Is there a God? Is this a punishment? What more could you have done? Your child does poorly in school. The teachers imply you aren't doing the right thing. More uncertainty. Your child becomes an adolescent. Besides the difficulty of watching a child become a sexually mature being, you face your own middle age. Uncertainty.

And because of your adolescent's changing thought processes, everything you say is challenged. Everything you believe is challenged. More uncertainty. It's amazing that most of us survive our children's adolescence without becoming abusive. Equally amazing is that our adolescents survive to become adults.

When uncertainty exists, the arousal it creates can be variously named. This is important, since naming the arousal helps you identify—and deal with—the feeling. If it can be easily resolved, the arousal can be best named "curiosity" or "interest." If it cannot be resolved, the arousal—and feeling—are more intense. For example, if the arousal seems to be created by another person, it becomes anger. If it seems to point to a flaw in your being, it becomes shame. If it seems to point to something you did or did not do, it becomes guilt. If it seems to have no cause, it becomes fear or anxiety. Unfortunately, the effort to resolve uncertainty can create more uncertainty, for when we don't know what to do, we seek advice.

Advice—Another Source of Uncertainty for Parents

Advice, particularly when it doesn't work, generates mountains of uncertainty. Everyone knows better than you how to raise your child. Everyone knows exactly what you should do to solve your current parenting problem, whether it involves colic, night terrors, temper tantrums, shyness, school problems, or teen problems. Moreover, everyone feels obligated to tell you where you are failing as a parent and to blame you for your child's problems. Everyone knows that if you don't follow their advice, you *want* your kids to be messed up, dysfunctional. Everyone knows that if following their advice doesn't help, you didn't do exactly what they told you to do.

Conflicting ideas about the right way to raise your children create uncertainty. Think of all the conflicting advice you have already had as a parent. One young mother I knew was driven to tears by the never-ending and well-meaning advice of strangers. Her daughter had an allergy that was not incapacitating but did leave the baby's skin peeling and dry. Everyone who saw the baby had one thing to say: "Get some lotion on that baby's face." But lotion was absolutely forbidden, since it was one source of the allergy. How many times in one hour could you explain that politely?

I taught this mother how to deal with the constant stream of advice. I helped her realize the problem was the uncertainty others created in her. She was a good mother, she was following the doctor's orders. She learned to say, "Thank you. I'll discuss your ideas with the baby's doctor."

She also learned to figure out when she wasn't able to deal with these kind of comments and to avoid exposure to these "advisers" by making do without shopping, getting someone else to do the shopping, or getting someone else to stay with her baby. If those things weren't possible, she did as little shopping as possible and carried her baby in a backpack, which meant the baby's peeling face and hands were not so visible. These strategies kept comments to a minimum.

Rules for Dealing with Advice

1. Remember: advice is a suggestion.

2. Tailor all advice to yourself, your situation, your child.

3. When someone is pressuring you to do things their way, stay calm and keep an open mind.

4. Experiment. Be a personal scientist. If something sounds reasonable, try it. If it works, great. If it doesn't work, try something else.

5. Remember: when advice doesn't work, you aren't to blame.

This chapter has talked about how feelings begin in general. A feeling begins in arousal, but it is only fully formed when named. Learning how your body tells you a feeling is starting and how you name feelings are important emotional fitness skills discussed in the next chapter.

3

Feeling
Awareness

Our body announces what we feel. If the signals were always clear, life would be easier. Unfortunately, sometimes a feeling gets mixed with other feelings, a physical arousal gets tangled with thoughts, one person's anger cue is another's sadness cue, or the same cue may stand for two different emotions. I cry just as easily when I am frustrated and angry as I do when I am sad.

Being aware of your and other people's feeling signals is a talent—one aspect of what Daniel Goleman, psychologist and writer, calls emotional intelligence. Reading feeling cues, either your own or someone else's, is an important part of feeling awareness. Not everyone is good at reading such cues. I remember knowing one of our foster children was lying just by the way she widened her eyes and looked right at me. Her probation officer didn't believe me.

"She's lying."

"Nonsense. What makes you think that?"

"Her face gets a funny wide-eyed look when she lies."

"Ah, you're doing a trip on the kid."

This was not a probation officer who thought highly of parents, so I didn't pursue my point. But later in the day proof that the girl was lying emerged. Reading feeling cues is a kind of talent some have more of than others, just like math skill, and, like math skill, it can be developed. Reading other people's feeling cues is important.

A client of mine had suffered many losses. Her husband walked out on her two days before their baby's first birthday. Ultimately, she had to move from a spacious home in the suburbs to a cramped city apartment. She had to leave a part-time job she loved for a full-time job she hated. When I first met her, not only did her face broadcast her sorrow, but her body frowned too. Anyone would have seen her pain. Eventually, I asked, "How does your body tell you about being sad?"

She sighed, a tear started, and she said, "I cry."

She was silent for a minute and then added, "My

throat hurts. I can't hold my head up, there is a sandbag on my back, and my shoulders want to fall down."

Loud signals. Signals she felt. Signals I saw.

Here's an exercise I use in my workshops to help improve awareness of how the body can communicate feeling cues. Like many of my exercises, it serves two purposes. Here, it makes you aware of how your body announces feelings. Ultimately, it becomes an exercise that can help you better control negative feelings.

Sad to Glad

Best done in a standing position, this exercise begins by assuming a "sad body" pose. Hang your head, droop your shoulders, feel all the losses of your life weighing you down. See how bleak everything looks. Imagine it is night. Sigh deeply. Notice the feelings this exercise creates in you. Most people find themselves feeling sadder than before doing the exercise.

Next, draw in a deep breath and imagine dawn is breaking. See the light beginning to shine down on you. As you breathe in and as the sun breaks through the darkness, think of a favorite arousing and inspiring song; hum or sing the song to yourself, straighten your shoulders, lift your head. Smile, keep singing the song, breathe out slowly, and feel the warmth of the sun filling your body. Breathe normally. Sing until the song is ended. Notice if "glad body" changes your feelings.

A lowered head, drooping shoulders, and a frown mean sadness across most cultures. A smile means pleasure; a grimace, pain. Each feeling produces its own bodily sensation and body language. Learning to be aware of feelings starts with being aware of how feelings feel.

READING SIGNALS

Feelings often get transferred quickly into bodily responses and behavior that can signal to us or others what it is we are feeling. Ask those who know you well how they can tell when you are feeling sad, mad, or bad.

Some signals are universal, some are person-specific. I am the youngest child in my family. The baby. One of my brothers, for the most part a good guy, loved to scare me. This brother was particularly adept at secreting himself in various nooks and crannies and then jumping out with a fearsome yell as I walked by.

When I am anxious, the first sign is a creepy feeling across my upper back. Yes, memories of the feeling I used to get after my brother had scared me or when I feared he was hiding somewhere. This creepy feeling is how my body tells me I am getting nervous or scared or worried about something.

I know I am getting angry when my jaw tightens and my eyes narrow. Another anger cue for me is a bodily sensation of wanting to strike out. I can best describe this sensation as little fists pushing along my shoulders and down my arms. Weird? Yes, but a signal nevertheless.

I asked David how his body told him when he was

getting angry. He said, "Tension in my chest and across my shoulders, and my throat tightens up."

As he spoke, he tightened his shoulders, hunched them forward, clenched his fists, and looked like a boxer ready to defend his title. Not only did his body send him a feeling message, he also did something that most other people would interpret as anger.

A former foster child of ours always signaled a pending temper storm by clenching and unclenching his fists. One father I worked with had a twitch in his right cheek that signaled disgruntled feelings about to break forth in one or more expletives.

Many bodily signals begin softly and build in intensity. The creeping feelings of fear I get when anxious often start softly, but if I get anxious enough my shoulders twitch. My anger almost always starts softly—just a tightening of my jaw. As my anger builds, other signals announce what is happening. But in learning to control my temper, I have learned to look for that first clenching of my jaw.

Body Signals for Most Common Feelings

Learning feeling cues helps you catch and control feelings while they are still controllable. Becoming aware of your specific feeling cues and learning to read other people's feeling cues accurately are major emotional fitness skills. A few of the major feelings and their cues are discussed below.

Fear. Common descriptions include: eyes widening; jaw dropping and mouth opening to form a small *o*; breath catching; heart stopping and then banging like a hammer; knees weakening; body trembling. Others report a sensation of blood draining from the face. Some feel dizzy or faint. Says one mom, "The doctor couldn't figure out what was wrong with the baby. I was terrified she was going to die. She was so pale and so lethargic. The whole time we were arranging her admission to the hospital, my heart was racing. I thought it was going to pound its way right out of my body."

Remember the last time you were afraid? Try to recreate the moment of fear in your mind. What body cues announced your fear? List those cues either in your mind or on paper and learn them, so that you can be aware of the specific feeling cues that tell you fear is starting.

Hurt or Sadness. Common descriptions include: eyes tearing; chin dropping or quivering; throat closing to hold back sobs; body folding in on itself; exhaustion; numbness. An example: "I couldn't move, I was so overcome. After my initial burst of tears, I shut off the pain, but I also had the feeling I was trapped in sand. Every movement took incredible effort. Just taking a breath seemed more than I could manage."

What are your specific body cues for announcing sadness? Learn them.

Anger. Common descriptions include: eyebrows pulling together; eyes narrowing, may fill with tears; lips and jaw tightening, scowling; head pounding; heart pounding;

breathing gets heavier; body tenses, trembles; hands become fists. Example: "When he said he hated me, I felt anger hit me like a sledgehammer. I could feel my eyes glazing over. My whole body seemed to tense up. It was gathering strength to retaliate. It's a good thing my husband got that kid out of the room as quickly as he did."

Learn and remember the clues that tell you anger is developing.

Guilt. Common descriptions include: eyes looking down; head hanging; mouth opening a little, lips turning down; a sinking sensation; stomach tightening; heart seeming caught in a vise; shoulders tensing as if warding off blows. Example: "Guilt beats me. That's the only way to describe it. Most of the blows fall on my back and shoulders. My body punishes me, no doubt about that. Do wrong, feel the stick."

I first thought this woman had been beaten during her childhood. She hadn't. She recalled only two spankings, but they had been on a well-padded bottom and more humiliating than painful. She also recalled that the sense of being beaten was related to a movie she saw in which a dog was beaten for growling back at his owner.

How does your body announce guilt? Learn the cues.

Shame. Most common descriptions include: cheeks flaming, body shrinking, eyes shifting down. Example: "We were sitting in the living room at our in-laws'. I was bouncing my son on my knee, something I've done hundreds of times. This time he got sick. I mean sick. I couldn't believe the amount of stuff that came out of his mouth. I also couldn't believe how embarrassed I was. The room got silent. My face got as hot as if I'd run a marathon. I thought my ears were going to burst into flame. I think it took two days for the blood to leave my face."

Note and remember how your body tells you shame or embarrassment is visiting you.

As with so many other experiences, how our body announces our feelings varies from person to person. There are no right and wrong signals—just signs you need to recognize. Learning to recognize these cues helps you build feeling awareness, and that is an important emotional fitness skill. Doing the following Body Scan exercise can help you spot the early signs that a feeling is developing.

Body Scan
By learning to scan your body for feeling cues, you will notice tensions and eventually connect those tensions to feelings.

Center yourself. (If you don't remember how, just take a deep calming breath and then breathe normally for the space of four breaths.)

When you are ready, create a "scanner." Your scanner can be anything that helps focus your attention on various parts of your body. Some people imagine a beam of light, others a magic wand. The scanner helps you examine your body from head to toe to see if you spot any feeling cues.

The important thing is to scan your entire body. This doesn't have to take long; you need to spend only a few seconds on each section: head, neck, shoulders, arms and hands, chest, lower trunk, legs, and feet. You can start with either your head or your feet.

Take a nice cleansing breath and go to work. Scan your body section by section. Focus your imaginary scanner; notice any tensions, numbness, or cold or hot feelings. Just notice it, name the sensation, and move on. When you have completed scanning all your body, take another deep breath, stretch, and think about what you have observed.

Here is the body scan I did as I wrote this:

I start with my toes. Nothing to notice there, but as I move up my legs, I feel the familiar end-of-the-day ache in my lower legs. I had rheumatic fever as a child and leg aches are a carryover. As I move up my body, my stomach says, "Isn't it time for a snack?" I put that one on hold. So far, all I am finding are physiologically based feelings. But as I move on, I find tension across my shoulders. I'm not certain what that is about. An end-of-the-day emotional pileup of some sort. And yes, right at the corners of my temples tiny fingers press, not enough to hurt, but enough to make me notice they are there—another sign something emotional is at work. Finally, it is hot, and I am also aware of spots of sweat and heat here and there.

The tension across my shoulders and the tiny fingers pressing against the corners of my temple demand further attention. The body scan made me aware that something is happening. The next step is figuring out what that something is. I concentrate on the tension and ask myself what is going on. As I do, the tension dissolves and my eyes momentarily fill with the hint of tears; my chest feels empty. Disappointment. Yes, that's it. It was a "down day." Very little that I did came to a positive end. Down days create tension.

I ask myself if there is something more going on. Nothing surfaces. Mostly, I am tired. I want things in my life to be further along than they are. I'm down because I want to stop working for the day and tense because I have lots to do and shouldn't stop for another hour or so. Maybe if I keep going, I can get something done. I'm pushing myself. Now that I know what I am feeling I am in the position to decide what I want to do. I can put the work away for the day; I can push on a bit longer. Whatever I decide, I own the feeling.

If you are a parent of young children, taking a time-out —stopping to rest or reflect—is not always an easy option. Not being able to stop makes it even more important to take a body scan every now and again. Managing feelings means being aware of them and taking action before they surge out of control.

Now it's your turn. Do a body scan. Notice which muscles are tense. Notice where the tension is strongest. Notice what parts of your body feel hot and what parts feel cold. Do you notice any tingling? Twitching? Do you feel blood rushing to or from any part of your body? How about pressure? Pain? Numbness?

"I was astounded," one woman told me. "I had never connected eating with anger until I did a body scan. I had just discovered my ten-year-old had been lying to me. I was enraged. I sat down to take a time-out and at the same time did a body scan. Well, once I moved past my pounding head, inflamed cheeks, and ready-to-yell throat, I discovered a hollow middle. I felt so empty and alone. No wonder I have a problem with my weight; I eat to fill the void anger creates."

Anger alienates. Alienation creates loneliness. Loneliness can feel like emptiness. Emptiness can feel like hunger. Feelings are bodily sensations. Bodily sensations help us name and understand our feelings.

Spend the next several days listening to your body. Do a quick body scan during the "wasted moments" I talked about earlier. Waiting in line? Do a body scan. Giving the baby a bottle? Do a body scan. A quick one takes only a minute and it is amazing what you will learn. As one woman who was skeptical commented: "Body scans. Ha. Well, I'll try anything once. So I did one after nursing the baby and before getting up to put him back in his crib. It was late and the house was quiet. The baby was sleeping quietly in my arms. Well, why didn't you tell me taking a body scan might pay off with good feelings? I knew I loved my baby, but just taking that minute to savor the feeling of him in my arms intensified all the good. I think it might be what a friend of mine calls 'being in the moment.' Yes, I was tired, and yes, I wanted to sleep, but I stayed there an extra ten minutes to savor the good feelings I discovered."

Body scans can alert you to good feelings as well as not so good ones. Try to do a body scan or two every day until you can do one in a few seconds. Those who practice taking a body scan often find they can eventually do a complete body scan in only one breath.

Feeling overwhelmed with all these exercises? Read more slowly. Master one exercise before reading the next. This is not a novel to be read once and only once. Nor is it intended to be a fast read. This is a book to read slowly, working your way through the exercises. It is a book to come back to and reread as needed. Yes, you can read it through quickly if that is your desire or style, but read it through and then go back and learn the exercises one by one.

NAMING WHAT WE FEEL

Feelings are intangible. You can't hold them or take pictures of them. Or pass them from hand to hand. When we name someone else's feelings, we examine their facial expressions, their body language, and their behavior; we listen to their words, we look at what else is going on, and only then can we make our best guess about what that person feels. Sometimes our best guess is wrong. And sometimes, when our best guess is about our own feelings, it can still be wrong. How often have you had the following conversation?

"You know you're angry. Admit it."

"Look, I'm depressed."

"Depression is anger turned inward."

"I'm not angry, I'm depressed. I know what I feel."

I hate being told I'm angry when I feel depressed. When the fog of depression disappears during a lightning flash of anger, I hate it even more. Unfortunately, sometimes we know what we feel; sometimes we don't.

Naming feelings is the process of separating black from gray, gray from white. Remember, arousals are just the beginning of a feeling; attaching the appropriate name to the arousal completes the birth of the feeling. Between the arousal and the name lies a vast land of opportunity.

William James, philosopher and educator, believed that feelings are individually determined. He believed this fact creates the possibility for a limitless number of emotions. Most American child-development theorists tend to see emotions in terms of a basic few: fear, anger, contempt, joy, sadness, disgust, excitement, surprise, guilt, and shame. Jerome Kagan, who agrees with James, points out that other cultures add emotions unnamed in America. Kagan notes in his book, *The Nature of the Child*, the following emotions other societies believe are as basic as fear or anger, joy or surprise:

amae—the Japanese word for a feeling of mutual interdependence with another.

nalik—the Utku Eskimo word for the feeling that accompanies wanting to nurture and protect another.

song—the word used by the Ifalukians of Micronesia for the feeling accompanying the recognition that another person has violated a community norm.

Thus, emotions have not only a personal meaning but a cultural meaning as well. When we learn to name feelings, we learn names specific to our culture and our family's particular interpretation of that culture. My parents, who were of Anglo-Saxon descent, believed that interrupting while someone was speaking was rude. My husband is Jewish; he was raised in a culture in which interrupting is a sign that you are paying attention and interested. This is an example of one behavior that leads to two different feelings depending on cultural and familial backgrounds. We learn to name our emotions in our parents' arms, and our parents transmit cultural values as a part of teaching us to name feelings.

As signals, feelings alert us and others to what is going on, but like all signals, feelings can get crossed. Daniel Stern, psychiatrist and professor at Cornell University, believes that the possibility of slippage—or inaccurately naming our or someone else's feelings—increases when we learn to speak and begin to rely on words to name our feelings. According to Stern, language's effectiveness rests on two minds forging an agreement as to what words mean. When feelings, which are abstract, are involved, agreement may be difficult: A child is angry. A parent has difficulty with expressions of anger. Instead of anger, she names what the child is feeling as hunger or fatigue or naughtiness. Or, a parent is very sad, but doesn't want her baby to know. She pretends to be happy, says how happy she is, but her baby senses this is a different feeling than the mother's normal happiness. Slippages. Failures to communicate. Shades of black forming a tangled mess.

The child whose parents fail to teach accurate names for feelings grows up either misnaming her feelings, not being able to accurately read someone else's feelings, or both. Feeling awareness means you are aware of your feelings and you can accurately name other people's feelings.

Naming and Observing a Feeling

Here's another exercise that helps develop your feeling awareness by encouraging you to name the feeling:

Take a minute to observe what you are feeling right now. Center, do a quick body scan. If any strong feeling cues are revealed, don't assume immediately that that is what is going on. Continue the body scan and at its end, take a deep abdominal breath. As you breathe out, ask yourself, "What feeling most fills me now?" Wait quietly for the feeling to announce itself. What if nothing happens? Observe what it feels like to look for a feeling and have nothing happen. See what that feels like. Feeling nothing is a feeling.

Whatever comes, name and greet it by saying "Hello." Even if it is a nothing feeling, greet it: "Hello, nothing feeling." For the space of one breath, observe what happens when you greet the feeling by name.

Next, frown and again observe what happens. Yes, even if the feeling you have named is a positive one, frown and observe the results. See what happens. Next, smile at the feeling. See what happens. Say goodbye to the feeling and see what happens.

Finally, take another long breath and center for a few breaths. Say a final goodbye to the feeling. Stretch, smile, and go on with what you were doing before.

This exercise accomplishes two things. It helps build feeling awareness, and the very process of stepping back and observing what is going on reduces the hold the feeling has on you. You own the feeling, it does not own you.

Naming Negative Feelings

When you are naming feelings, it is usually best to accept the first name that comes. But, when a feeling seems to be demanding a hurtful action on your part or involves negative reactions to your children's feelings, you should take some time to check out exactly what this feeling is and why you are feeling it.

The same behavior in a child can create differently named feelings in different adults. Often parents describe to me their response to a cranky and overtired child who at some point during the day tells the parent, "I hate you." Here are how some have responded to those words:

One parent felt outrage: *"No child of mine is going to sass me back. Saying he hates me is intolerable."*

Another parent felt guilt: *"I wasn't sensitive enough. I should have been more caring."*

A third parent responded with shame: *"I'm a terrible mother."*

Each parent faced the same arousing event—a tired and sassy child. Each felt something when the child hurled the words "I hate you." Each named and handled what they felt differently based on his or her own history. The outraged parent came from a family and culture that believes the measure of respect shown by a child to a parent is a measure of the parent's worth. When Sassy and Tired Child lashed out, the child's words were a chain saw ripping through that parent's self-esteem.

The guilty parent didn't believe getting angry was acceptable. Getting angry at a tired child is a major sin. Guilt often results as a response to an anger we feel is inappropriate or can't be expressed.

The parent who felt shame had been abused as a child. Every time anyone was angry, this parent felt she was to blame.

Once the brain attaches a name to a feeling, the why comes into play. With Sassy and Tired Child two whys have to be asked: "Why am I getting angry?" and "Why is he behaving this way?" As noted above, the why was different for each parent. Asking why the child is behaving the way he is leads to the only appropriate way to handle Sassy and Tired Child's behavior. The appropriate response to the negative feelings and the child's behavior would be: "He's tired. I can't take such talk seriously. The important thing is to get him to bed." When Sassy and Tired child is sleeping, the parent's negative feelings should subside.

HOW FEELINGS END

Feelings don't just go on and on. Marsha Linehan, a psychologist and professor at the University of Washington, notes that, given the way the brain is structured, most feelings should fade in seconds. However, as you have probably noticed, some feelings seem to go on forever. Linehan says this happens because something keeps "refiring" the feeling. In one way or another, the feeling has not been dealt with effectively. By Linehan's thinking, it seems that feelings can end in just one of three ways:

1. Feelings end when acted on in such a way that the feeling is no longer needed. Hungry? Eat a meal and the hunger fades. Angry? Act on the anger and calm down.

2. Feelings end when another feeling overtakes and overpowers the first. For example, this is what happens when angry feelings replace sexual feelings.

3. Most feelings eventually fade away even if not expressed. This is called habituation and means that we get used to something and the "feeling" fades as a signal needing immediate attention.

The process of establishing control over negative feelings begins with your knowing when a feeling is starting, being able to observe it, and naming it properly. When you are aware of a negative feeling, you can sometimes slow down its growth. This can only be done if you start the process of dampening the feeling before it reaches the danger zone. Feeling awareness helps with that process. So does being able to measure the growth of negative feelings.

4

Measuring Feelings

We don't always know what we feel. We may not feel angry, but others may see the anger building. Learning to be aware of feelings as soon as they begin and then learning to measure their growth helps us stay in control. We stay in control by taking action early in the growth of a negative feeling. Waiting too long puts the feeling in charge. Once negative feelings reach a certain point in their growth cycle, they acquire a life of their own. Daniel Goleman alludes to this when he says intense emotions hijack reason. When emotion hijacks reason, the feeling owns the person.

The more accurately you can measure the growth of negative feelings, however, the more you own those feelings. If you own your feelings they are objects; you can look at them, examine them, control them, turn them off and on. You are in charge. If a feeling owns you, you are that feeling's object—the feeling controls you.

Think of a child afraid of the dark and of going to sleep alone in a dark room. Fear of the dark can overtake a child. According to Robert Kegan, psychologist and Harvard professor, children are "embedded" in their feelings. Think of a seed in the middle of a flower pot. The potting mixture owns the seed: all the seed knows of the outside world comes from the potting mixture. When embedded in a feeling, a child cannot look at the feeling. When a child is afraid of the dark, he cannot see it or separate from it. The feeling surrounds and engulfs the child.

When a child wakes in the middle of the night, certain a monster is lurking in the dark, his fear creates the monster. But to the child, the monster creates his fear. All your wise explanations don't help. As one of my children said to me, "The monster knows to hide from you. If you leave, the monster will just come back."

Albert Ellis, a psychologist and the theorist behind Rational Emotive Therapy, calls such thinking Emotional Reasoning. This is expected when it comes to children, but not expected of adults. Growing up involves gradually becoming more and more able to own your feelings instead of being owned by them. Learning to take a feeling temperature helps you better own negative feelings. When you own a feeling, you are in charge.

TAKING YOUR CURRENT FEELING TEMPERATURE

Measure what you are feeling right now. First, give whatever you are feeling the simplest possible name. Try "feels good" or "feels bad." Next, think about how good or how bad. On a scale of one to ten, use one for terrible, ten for wonderful, and five for in between. As you do this, you are taking your feeling temperature, and you are creating a personal feeling thermometer. Just as you take your child's temperature to measure a fever's growth, you take a feeling temperature to measure a feeling's growth. You give your child Tylenol during the early stages of a fever to keep it from rising; you take feeling temperatures to determine if you need to take corrective action to keep feelings from reaching the point where emotion overrides reason. You want to slow the growth of a negative feeling before it reaches the point of no return—the point when control is lost.

Here are the complete instructions for taking a feeling temperature:

First, decide which feeling you want to measure. Anger? Fine. Measure anger on an "erupting" scale. Ten is the boil-over or exploding point; one is cool and calm. Remember the times you got so angry you did something you regret—something that hurt someone you cared for, or that damaged property, or that landed you in legal difficulties? Pick the worst. That is ten on your anger feeling thermometer.

For my ten, there's the time I yelled at the baby and banged on the mattress in rage. Another ten ended with me half slapping one of my kids across the face. (I saw what was happening and pulled back so that the slap was a graze. Not an action I am happy remembering.) There is also the time I threw a spoon at David. But that is more like an eight. He thinks I missed by accident, but I have better aim than he realizes.

You've identified your ten. Now find your one. Remember a time when you were so calm you couldn't be ruffled by a strong wind. Days by the ocean calm me, so my one is sitting on the sand alone at sunset, watching the gulls, the sandpipers, and the waves.

Now find your five. Five means anger has arrived but is still manageable. I know my five—I feel offended or hurt; someone is doing something to me that I don't think I deserve. Resentment is the six on my anger scale, and it is the clue that if I don't take action to thwart the anger, the anger will hijack reason. I will end up doing things I regret. Anything I do when my anger is at a seven, eight, nine, or ten only makes things worse.

Six is the gateway into my danger zone and is when I need to take a time-out before doing anything more. I know I am at six when I begin asking resentment-based questions: Why am I doing what the other person should be doing? Why isn't the other person grateful? Does he think I'm stupid or a fool? If I don't pay attention to my resentment, I become more and more angry and raging. So, on my feeling thermometer, resentment is a sign to take charge of the anger before it takes charge of me.

Don't Be a FAT Head

The purpose of a feeling thermometer is to identify when to begin dampening a dangerously intensifying feeling so you can take appropriate action before the feeling takes over. When I am working with kids, I speak of the importance of not becoming a FAT head. A FAT head is someone who Feels, Acts, and only then, Thinks. Children were born to be FAT heads and need help learning to think before they act. Grown-ups are supposed to feel, think, and then act. Thinking before acting on a feeling is what feeling management is all about.

Some grown-ups never act without thinking, but most of us at one time or another act on negative feelings and wish we had thought more clearly beforehand about what to do. I use the slogan "Under stress we regress" to remind myself and students that, given enough stress, anyone can slip into thinking emotionally instead of rationally. The trick to thinking first is to know when your feelings are beginning to take over.

If I take time to think when I hit five or six on my feeling thermometer, I can keep my resentment from turning to rage. Four, five, and six are usually pivotal points on anyone's feeling thermometer. You want to identify many feeling cues to help you know when you are reaching the point when a feeling might begin to control you. A feeling cue a sign or signal that a certain feeling is at a particular point. The following feeling cues tell me I've reached a five or six on my anger thermometer:

I feel resentment.

My jaw gets tense.

My shoulders get tense.

I begin talking to myself about how unfair the other person is being. I suggest that they must think I am their slave. (I learned this kind of self-talk from my mother. She learned it from her mom. Just a day or two ago one of my sons asked if I thought he was my slave. Ancestral self-talk lives on! However, my son smiled when he used these words on me, proving he is further along the emotional maturity scale than I am.)

If I am doing something—cooking dinner, for example—I start banging things around.

I start telling myself how stupid and foolish I am, how I should know better, how I didn't think or was naive, or that the other person thinks I'm foolish. (As I am writing this I feel my eyes narrow.)

I see myself taking revenge. I start my plan to make the other person suffer.

These cues tell me to take a break, chill out, or soak my hands in ice water, and if that doesn't calm me down, to bury my head in ice cubes. (OK. I don't really bury my head or soak my hands. I do wash my face with cold water sometimes. Marsha Linehan suggests that soaking your hands or holding ice cubes can help calm you down. Chilling out has more than one meaning.)

A FEELING THERMOMETER FOR ANGER

my feeling temperature	*my feeling cues*
10 ————➤	Acting on rage. Yelled at baby. Crying.
9 ————➤	Raging. Name-calling. Seeing red.
8 ————➤	Angry. Thinking this is awful. Jaw tense.
7 ————➤	Resentful. Thinking others are mistreating me.
6 ————➤	Irritated. Wondering why I am such a patsy.
5 ————➤	Annoyed. Thinking others should have behaved better.
4 ————➤	Offended. Mild hurt; feeling taken advantage of.
3 ————➤	OK. I can do this; I like helping others.
2 ————➤	Calm. Life is a A-OK.
1 ————➤	Calmest. Life is a day at the beach.

What about the other numbers on the thermometer? Filling them in refines your feeling thermometer. As discussed, resentment is my six. When I begin snapping at the other person, I'm moving into my seven. Beginning to feel as if I am going to jump out of my skin is eight. At nine I see red, and that is just one number away from rage. When raging, I strike out. I also cry.

Things I need to do when my feeling temperature for anger enters the danger zone: *Think.* Stop trying to help. Stop talking. Stop suggesting solutions. Remind myself I can say no to others. Remind myself to say no, but gently and politely. Remind myself to center, breathe through my abdomen, and count my breath.

CREATING A PERSONAL FEELING THERMOMETER

The chart on page 58 is my own feeling thermometer for my angry feelings. To create your own personal feeling thermometer, remember the feeling at its most intense. Then recall a time when it didn't exist and, finally, find a point midway between the two. The most important cues are the ones that cluster around five. At a minimum, try to get in touch with a number of different cues for your five. Ask yourself the following questions:

1. What does my body tell me is happening at a five? If I did a body scan, what cues would I discover?

2. What other feelings are around at the time? What do I feel before and after the feeling being measured?

3. What variations of the feeling in question can I identify?

4. Does my behavior change as my feeling thermometer moves toward the danger zone? Do I begin pacing, talking faster or louder, pounding my fist, tearing paper?

5. How could someone else tell what I was feeling?

6. What do I say to myself about what is happening?

Using the blank chart on page 64, make up your own thermometer. If you cannot recall any useful cues from memory, go through the six questions again. It might take several tries to develop the thermometer, but when you finally determine the feeling cues that will help you know when you're moving toward the danger zone, you will be in better control of your feelings.

MEASURING SHUT-DOWN FEELINGS

Some emotions dull us, rendering us almost immobile. The emotions that I teach people to measure on such a shut-down scale are sadness and its cousin depression, and guilt and its cousin shame. These emotions suggest restraint rather than action.

FEELING THERMOMETER FOR DEPRESSION

feeling temperature	feeling cues
10	Ecstatic. Tell myself things couldn't be better.
9	Great. Everything is going really well.
8	Good. Taking care of my baby and me.
7	OK. Occasional doubts and low moments.
6	Good/bad. Can't take time for me; feel guilty.
5	Pressured. Feeling over-whelmed, heavy.
4	Down. Don't get dressed. Eating chocolate.
3	Tired. Do as little as possible but still tired.
2	Ugly. Think my baby is out to get me. Sleep.
1	The end. I can't go on. Running away.

On page 61 is a feeling thermometer created by a young mother who suffered from postpartum depression. This is a depression thermometer and is measured on a falling, or shut-down, scale. Ten is wonderful. One is her personal low.

Clearly, this mom's major clue to a depression getting out of control is isolating herself, seeing herself as a bad mother, and giving up on taking care of her own needs. Feeling "heavy" is a strong body cue. The fact that she cannot take off an hour a day to do something for herself is another prime indicator. She needed some counseling and support to get back on track, but learning to take a feeling temperature helped her regain control.

"Funny," she said to me the day we said goodbye, "I hated the idea of a feeling thermometer. I didn't tell you at the time, but I thought it was just a lot of psychobabble. It wasn't. I think what helped most was realizing that I had a hundred different feelings a day, and that just five minutes after feeling perfectly horrible, I could be at a ten. Feelings do come and go."

It is not necessary to develop a detailed feeling thermometer for all feelings. The trick is to get in the habit of taking a quick feeling temperature off and on during the day. Without knowing it, you already take half a feeling thermometer lots of times a day. Think about how many times you've thought the following during any given day:

"Feeling on top of things."

"Going out of my mind."

"Boring."

"I'm really down in the dumps."

Every time you make a statement like this, you are taking a feeling temperature. When someone asks me how I feel, I use it as a reminder to do a quick body scan, to observe my feelings, and to take my feeling temperature. I do that even when I know and reply automatically that I am fine. When someone asks how you are, do the same and you've practiced feeling awareness and feeling measuring. Both are important emotional fitness skills.

If you want to take a closer look at one specific feeling, then concentrate on measuring that feeling. If anger is a troubling emotion for you, measure your anger. If the blues are getting you down, measure sadness. Use the feeling thermometer chart on page 64 as a guide.

TIME-OUT

Sometimes just taking a feeling temperature and doing some breath counting is enough to reverse the flow of negative feelings. However, if your feeling temperature continues to move into the danger zone, you probably need to take a time-out. A time-out is just what it says —time to think about what to do next. While sports time-outs are short, yours don't have to be. Your job is to stay in time-out until calm. When calm, you can think about what to do next.

YOUR FEELING THERMOMETER

This feeling thermometer will measure _____ .
List as many feeling cues as you can. Then underline the
ones that indicate your feeling is moving toward the danger
zone. These are the cues that cluster around five. These are
the cues that will help you take a time-out before the feeling
overwhelms and takes charge of you.

your feeling temperature   *your feeling cues*

10 ⟶

9 ⟶

8 ⟶

7 ⟶

6 ⟶

5 ⟶

4 ⟶

3 ⟶

2 ⟶

1 ⟶

Things I must do when my feelings move into the danger zone:
_____
_____
_____
_____

Of course, parents can't always take a time-out. That's why parents need to learn self-soothing skills and to develop a calming program. I'll talk more about self-soothing and calming down in the next few chapters. Right now, remember that the sooner such skills are brought into play the more likely you will control the feeling. Learning to spot the need to take either a time-out or to begin using other self-soothing skills is important.

LOOKING FOR PATTERNS

Keeping a daily log of feeling temperatures helps you spot negative feeling patterns. On page 66 is a brief form, called a feeling log, that you can use to spot patterns as well as improve your general feeling awareness. You should use this form in conjunction with the Body Scan, Naming and Observing a Feeling, and the Feeling Thermometer exercises. While keeping the log, note anything else you think is important and that relates to the feeling. Some of the things to think about are physiologically based arousals, who is around, and self-talk related to the feeling. When you note the intensity of the feeling, also note the cues that helped you identify the intensity. Keep the log for a week if possible.

If keeping a log sets your teeth on edge, don't keep one. To the very orderly, keeping a diary or a log comes almost naturally, but others of us are more inclined to haphazardness. We find the idea of keeping a diary im-

possible. So try it and if you can do it, fine. If you aren't
a diary or log keeper, try to keep at least an informal eye
in patterns of feelings.

FEELING LOG

date	feeling name	feeling scale	describe situation
time 1		1–2–3–4–5–6–7–8–9–10	
time 2		1–2–3–4–5–6–7–8–9–10	
time 3		1–2–3–4–5–6–7–8–9–10	
time 4		1–2–3–4–5–6–7–8–9–10	

LOOKING FOR ARSENIC HOURS

A point of keeping a feeling log or an eye out for patterns is to help you become aware of what some call the arsenic hours of life. Arsenic hours are regularly occurring times of difficulty. Here's one mother's description of an arsenic hour.

> I once read a newspaper story about a family who had a fancy breakfast three mornings a week. These "family breakfasts" substituted for the missed family dinners caused by the children's overcrowded schedules. Everyone got up an hour earlier than usual those days. According to the article, these breakfasts were quality family time. I wanted to gag. I consider my mornings a success if no blood is drawn and no bones broken. My kids are not morning people and that is that. They're great kids when they come home from school and until they go to bed at night. But they're Hell's Angels during the first two or three hours of their day.

When I told her I and others call such times arsenic hours, this mom was able to laugh and gain some perspective. She faced facts: all the organization in the world wasn't going to turn her kids into smiling bundles of joy at dawn's early light. Together, this mom and I went on a search to make the mornings somewhat less lethal. We came up with the following strategy:

1. *Take showers at night and have the two boys wear sweats to bed that can be worn to school.* Some mornings the boys decided to put on jeans, other mornings it was roll out of bed, don sneakers, and stumble to the car—their choice. Some might find this unacceptable. But this mother was not that fastidious and, if you really think about it, how dirty do sweats get between clean sheets? The nights before she had gym class, her daughter also wore sweats to bed.

2. *Take along breakfasts.* The kids were happier eating in the car than sitting around the table glowering at each other. For the daughter, this meant eating the same thing for breakfast that she ate for lunch. She liked it that way. Peanut butter sandwiches, bananas, milk, and one chocolate chip cookie were her favorites. If permitted, that would have been her dinner as well. Letting her have her way with this kept her from whining and Mom from exploding. For the other two kids, eat-on-the-way breakfast meant a piece of fruit, a cardboard carton of milk, and two breakfast bars. One ate in the car, the other during recess. Mom packed breakfast when she made the lunches.

3. *Every evening when homework time is done, have the kids gather everything needed for school the next day, put it in their school bags, and put the*

school bags in the family station wagon. Come morning, they could dash to the car. They only needed to remember to keep their heads on and grab their lunches and breakfast bags.

4. *Find acceptable ways to communicate early in the morning.* The kids didn't want to talk or be talked to—common when your body thinks it is still sleeping. Mom was a morning person and liked to chatter. Too often, the chattering turned to nagging. The kids asked her not to talk to them. She agreed to use pantomime and hand signals as long as there was forward movement toward getting out of the house.

5. *No television.* The kids would and did zone out on television instead of doing what had to be done. Mom agreed not to talk; the kids agreed not to watch television.

6. *Call on neutral third parties for help.* For this family, a timer was set to go off five minutes before it was time to leave. Generally, at this point, Mom got her coat on and headed for the car. Another louder timer announced car-departure time.

7. *Set consequences for laggards.* If the laggards meant another child would be late for school, Mom simply left the laggards at home to find their own way to school. Being late for school

meant being grounded a day for each half an hour of lateness.

Because Mom was a morning person and wanted to chat, she had a little difficulty with the no-talk rule, but eventually she learned to sit herself down, enjoy an extra cup of coffee, and listen to a favorite CD while the kids soaked up every last possible Z.

Did these strategies work? More often than not. This arsenic hour became an aspirin hour—difficult, but not lethal.

Bedtime is another common arsenic hour. A father's lament: "From the time we signal time for bed until our daughter finally konks out, the urge to poison or at least drug our precious bundle of joy runs dangerously high." This bedtime arsenic hour family had also done most of what the traditional advice givers had suggested. You know the routine:

Staying-in-Bed Rules

1. A consistent bedtime

2. A consistent bedtime routine

3. A reward system for good bedtime behavior

4. Ignoring attention-seeking calls and cries of distress

5. Proper punishment for out-of-bed behaviors

A little detective work on my part uncovered one important fact. The little girl involved in this nightly struggle had shown signs of not needing a great deal of sleep. She had given up her morning nap at nine months and all naps by the time she was eighteen months.

Now, some people, children included, need less sleep than other people. (I do nicely on five or six.) Apparently, this little one didn't need a great deal of sleep, and this family's arsenic hour faded when Needs-Little-Sleep Daughter was allowed to play quietly in her room until she fell asleep. She had to go to her room, but could color or read or listen to music until she felt sleepy, as long as she was quiet and didn't come out of her room. Her parents never quite knew when their darling daughter fell asleep, but the toxicity of this arsenic hour had been significantly reduced. She always woke up when her parents first called her, a sure sign she had gotten enough sleep.

Arsenic Hour Survival Rules

To get yourself through those tough times of the day, try to follow these survival tips:

1. Reduce all expectations to a minimum. Do what can be done to prepare for the arsenic hour beforehand. Put off anything that can be put off.

2. Divide up as much of the absolutely essential work as possible.

3. Set up rewards for things that get done the right way.

4. Set up punishments for unacceptable behavior.

5. Practice Counting Your Breath (see pages 9–10).

6. When the dreaded hour is over, congratulate yourself and have a cup of tea or other soothing drink.

ONE-NOTE FEELINGS

Regularly taking a feeling temperature and keeping a feeling log may also alert you to more than arsenic hours. Other patterns may come to light. For example, some feelings don't come and go. If you find you are locked into the same feeling, you should take note. When the feeling is a negative one like anger, sadness, fear, or guilt, worrying is appropriate.

Also worry if the feeling is always a steady "nothing" without any ups or downs. This could mean you are numbed. Feeling numb is not good. Numb is limiting— you know no pain and you know no joy—unless, of course, you are a Buddhist monk and have found the enlightenment of detachment. But I am told even the Dalai Lama knows moments of anger.

And yes, I know some people are not full of feelings. Some people are "low reactors." Feelings just don't impact them the way they do other people. Just as different people have different thresholds when it comes to physical sensations, the same is true when it comes to emotions. Low reactors and high reactors sometimes marry each other. The more passionate one feels soothed by the calm the low reactor radiates, while the calm one feels energized by the high reactor.

If every time you take your feeling temperature, you hit a five, it is possible you have been endowed with low reactivity and are not numbed out. Take a five-minute life scan to double-check this. You aren't looking for lots of details, just variations in feelings or the lack of them. Scanning my life I see happiness until age six or seven, loneliness from seven to eleven, and mixed emotions from the time I was twelve until I fell in love at sixteen. So it would go right up to now. If I divide my life into ten-year periods, the scan is faster. The results are clear: I am not a low reactor.

Look for highs and lows. If you feel few over the long haul, but also have a sense that you and your life are okay, you are probably a low reactor and not numbed out. Being numbed out usually involves feeling empty and hopeless—not OK. A low reactor feels OK but has few, if any, emotional roller-coaster rides during the course of his or her life. The other kids may have whooped it up on Christmas day, whereas a low reactor was quietly happy; a low reactor faced with a big test didn't blink; if the school football team won the state championship, a low reactor smiled while the rest of the school rioted. A low reactor thinks other people are too emotional but has learned to put up with it. If all this fits you, you have low reactivity.

If, on the other hand, you know that once upon a time you bubbled with laughter, boiled with anger, dripped with tears, and shivered with fright, and now all you feel is a steady lack of reaction, numbness is the more distinct possibility. Numbness is what happens when life clobbers your nervous system. Numbness is good in helping combat pain so you can do what you have to do. But what is useful for a quick spurt of pain relief during a crisis becomes counterproductive in the long run. Numbness eats energy. Numbness destroys the good with the bad. No pain, no joy.

If you think you have numbed-out, get help. You deserve better than going through life with your feelings on hold or shut down. Finish reading this book and practice the exercises, but also find a good therapist.

Other one-note feelings exist. Anger is one, guilt another, depression a third. If every time you take a feeling temperature you find only one of these three, you also probably need more help then a book can deliver. Try my suggestions, particularly the exercises devoted to feeling awareness, but also get help. Life can be better.

5

Creating a Personal

Self-soothing

Program

Taking a feeling temperature so you know just when to take a time-out helps you calm down. Staying calm is an important emotional fitness skill, and you need to learn techniques to calm yourself and avoid others' interference. This chapter shows you how to build a personal self-soothing program using a number of relaxation or meditation exercises, including ones I have already discussed.

HOW REACTIVE ARE YOU?

I talked a little about reactivity levels in the previous chapter. Low reactors don't get stressed the way high reactors do. If you are a low reactor you almost always think before you act, you don't get easily upset, and you don't need this book to help you calm down. On the other hand, you may need help understanding why your child or your child's other parent gets so upset sometimes. Low reactors see high reactors as hysterical. This book will help you be more understanding of those who react strongly to feelings.

High reactors respond intensely to all sorts of arousals, including thoughts. A high reactor can think anger and get angry. They think calm and get calm. Because relaxation exercises involve being able to respond intensely to thoughts, if you are a high reactor you find the right relaxation exercise very helpful and this book can be very helpful to you.

Most of you are between these two extremes. For most people, self-soothing or relaxation or meditation programs ultimately work under two conditions: if the program is tailored to fit, and if the program is practiced religiously. Before moving on to creating a personal program, let me say another word or two about practicing.

DEVELOPING YOUR AUTOMATIC KNOWLEDGE

I have been telling you repeatedly to practice, practice, practice. I wish I could stop repeating this mantra. I can't; it is too important. Practice enough and a self-soothing program will work automatically. Automatic knowledge results from programming the brain. Automatic brain programs include information about such things as walking, talking, and riding a bicycle—you don't have to think about how to talk, you just talk. The more you do something, the sooner it gets programmed into the brain and becomes automatic knowledge. I designed my self-soothing exercises so that each can be practiced quickly and easily in order to speed up the programming process. Even so, they must be practiced and practiced and practiced before they become automatic.

A father once came to me asking for help. He was particularly concerned about the frequency with which he was blowing up at his nine-year-old son. He remembered his own father yelling at him, and the memory was not a good one. He had also already tried some relaxation exercises and so didn't have a lot of faith in mine. He was an avid basketball player, however, and when I told him what I just told you, he acknowledged how important it was to practice, practice, practice. As he told me, "Larry Bird practiced harder than anyone else on his team even after he became a star for the Boston Celtics. He'd be in the gym when the others went home, and he'd be there before the others showed up."

This dad understood the importance of practicing.

We worked together and designed a program just for him, which he practiced for ten minutes when he got up in the morning, after eating lunch, and at night before falling asleep. He practiced during every waste moment that came his way. Instead of flipping channels during commercials, he practiced his self-soothing program. At boring meetings, he practiced. About four or five weeks after I started working with him, he came and reported the following:

> Yesterday I came home tired and ready to kill. My kid met me at the door whining about how mean his sister was being. I said to myself, "Nothing has changed." Then I took a feeling temperature and I was at an eight, going on explode. Next, I took a deep breath, trying to get enough air to let him have it. He's too old to be running to Daddy, I thought. As I was breathing in, I found myself saying that stupid phrase you taught me to help slow down the growth of a negative feeling. "Breathing in," then "Breathing out," and then "Smiling." And as I made that stupid little half-smile of yours, I knew I was going to take a time-out. I just put my hand up, made a time-out sign, and walked straight to a comforting hot shower. By the time I had dried myself off and changed my clothes, my feeling temperature had dropped to a more serene three. What seemed like the end of the world had become just one of the annoying parts of being a dad—the price I pay for the good times.

Until the exercises began to work, this father wasn't convinced practicing would pay off in the same way practicing his jump shot would. He agreed to give it six weeks, and he practiced every chance he got. It worked. The program we designed for him became as easy to recall as taking a deep, cleansing breath. "I never would have made it if the practicing hadn't been so easy," he told me. "I really wasn't sure, but figured I had nothing to lose and a lot to gain."

If this were a scholarly book, I could list pages of references documenting how Counting Your Breath or any of the other exercises I teach derive from a scientific understanding of how feelings come to be and, therefore, how they can be best managed. All the studies show that being able to step back from a feeling, to calm down, is the most important part of feeling management strategies. The studies also show that it takes lots of repetition to create the kind of automatic program needed to calm down when things around you are heating up.

TAILORING YOUR SELF-SOOTHING EXERCISES

The studies also support the idea that self-soothing or relaxation exercises need to be tailored to fit each individual. Each of us is unique, we can't be cloned. Practicing is very important, but so is creating a personal self-soothing program attuned to your needs.

Visualization is one of the most common forms of self-soothing exercises (visualizing is seeing a tropical beach or imaging yourself somewhere serene and calming). If you don't visualize well, visualizations can annoy and frustrate you. But most people learn best visually, which is why visualizations are a popular form when it comes to relaxation exercise. Some people can visualize scenes from any book they've read. They read it once, and whenever they want to remember something from it, these superstars of visualization flip through the pages in their minds until they find what they need.

Do you win spelling contests? Most likely, you are a visualizer. You see and think in pictures. Lucky you; after all, one picture is worth a thousand words. Good spellers see the letters pop up on a screen in their minds, and then they either sound or sense that the words are right. Those who sound out the letters they see are probably the best spellers.

Another common form of self-soothing exercise is tense-and-release. Tense a muscle group and then relax the same muscle group. Tense-and-release exercises work best for people who learn by doing. None of the usual self-soothing exercises worked for me until I figured out how to adapt each to the way my brain works. This was frustrating at the time, but it did help me develop lots of different exercises and taught me the importance of helping people create their own exercise. The ecological theorists speak of a "goodness of fit" when talking about such things. Goodness of fit can refer to things as diverse as dressing properly for the climate, or planting the right seeds in the right soil, or the impact of a child's personality on a parent. When thinking about calming your body's response to a negative emotion, you need to find a personal goodness of fit with the various exercises used in this book. Next, you need to layer or combine the various exercises that work for you into a powerful program.

THE POWER OF LAYERING

Mark Katz, a psychologist and the director of the Learning Center in San Diego, California, makes the point that most teachers teach the way they learn. This is great for the kids who learn the same way the teacher learns, but not so great for other kids. The best teachers use all three modes when teaching. They present visual material and auditory material and underscore it all with some bodily movement. This is called layering.

Layering also involves bringing together a number of different memories. The first time I experienced the power of layering different sensory paths came about accidentally. Here's how: when I was a foster parent, I would often jog after dinner. I have a particular fondness for the sky at dusk, and exercise is always calming. When I jogged, I always listened to the same recording of Beethoven. I hummed to the music as I jogged. I also always followed the same route. This particular route took me up a hill. At the top of the hill were a lovely tree and a small grove of pine trees. As I reached the top of the hill, the adrenaline rush always kicked in when I saw the tree silhouetted against the sky and smelled the pine grove. I followed this pattern for days and days.

One day, I was tense and couldn't run. I remember wishing I could. I started humming Beethoven and seeing myself jogging out of the house. I ended up taking the run in my mind. I followed my usual route, "saw" the dusk-filled sky, kept on humming Beethoven's music, and when I reached the tree and "smelled" the pine grove, I felt a surge of calmness and joy. Powerful. I had learned to use these layered memories as a calming program.

As I am writing this, the memory strengthens, and all I have to do is hum Beethoven's music and I can feel a surge of energy and joy.

Your ultimate goal is to develop a self-soothing exercise that you can use anytime, anywhere. I have practiced and developed my calming program to the point where one calming breath combined with a sentence or two describing the pine grove calms me. Humming a bar or two of Beethoven adds more strength.

Creating a Safe Place

My calming jog is not the only way I calm down. I also use one or another of my safe places.

Creating a safe place adds another layer of intensity to your self-soothing program. The most powerful safe places call on memories of actual calming events and times. Those memories are already embedded in your brain, and using them to create your safe place strengthens the power of all your self-soothing exercises. The more positive memories you can use in building your safe place, the better.

When I want to get really calm I go to one of my safe places. I have a number of safe places, but you don't need to create more than one.

My jogging memory is an example of how to use a memory as a self-soothing program. But it is a safe jog, not a safe place. One of my safe places is the loft of a stable. Because I don't visualize easily, I describe this scene to myself: I am lying in a soft pile of straw, a kitten lies next to me softly purring, and at my feet, several dogs sleep and dream. The loft is dark and full of blue shadows, but through an open door, I can see the bright blue, sunlit sky. White, fluffy clouds drift by. It is the middle of a hot summer afternoon. The loft, however, is not hot. An occasional breeze blows softly across my face. The horses are in their stalls, flies buzz, and an occasional barn swallow darts by overhead. The smells of the stable are many and comforting. No one else is around. My safe place stable was created from memories of various stables I rode from and worked in during my teens and twenties.

Another safe place I visit has been created from a number of different memories put together. In this one, I am sitting in a rocking chair on the porch of a log cabin. The cabin sits on the edge of a lake in the midst of a pine forest. Across the lake, a beautiful snow-topped mountain rises. The cabin and lake are built from memories of two places, one in a pine wood in upstate New York; the other, a rustic camp in Connecticut. The rocking chair is one from my childhood. The snowcapped mountain is Mt. Mansfield, viewed from Burlington, Vermont.

Now it is your turn. Review your good-memory file

for peak experiences of calm and pleasure. See or describe those places. See each place in as much detail as possible. Change any unpleasant features. Add sounds. Add some music. Actually humming the music might help intensify the experience. What smells do you associate with each place? Where are you sitting or lying? What is the air temperature? Add to this place whatever will comfort and calm you. This is your creation. Combine aspects of each place.

Creating my safe place took months. Every time I tried to create the perfect place something was wrong and I'd start worrying about getting things perfect. This is not useful. Eventually I relaxed, focused on what worked, and bit by bit I put together my various safe places. You can do the same.

Creating a Viewing Screen

Once you have created your safe place, add a viewing screen. Later, the viewing screen will serve a number of useful purposes; for now the viewing screen lets you look from one safe place to another safe place. This is another way to layer and intensify the impact of a self-soothing exercise. You may find this idea confusing at first. It may not sound much different from what I have just taught you, but it is. What I want you to do is to *add* a viewing screen to your safe place so you can go to your safe place, put up your viewing screen, and see yourself in your safe place. I go to my stable and look at my viewing screen and see myself rocking on the front porch of my cabin in the woods.

When creating a viewing screen, it is always best to use something that blends into the serenity of the place. The wall of the barn. A cloud floating above in the sky. A picture on a wall. A movie screen. Still, your screen is your screen and you should make it what will work for you. If you don't visualize easily, the screen won't be as useful to you. You will need to tell yourself what you see on the screen. That is essentially what I have to do. I don't see my barn or the log cabin. I tell myself about it:

"There I am lying in the barn loft, petting my cat, the dogs are at my feet, it is hot, and I am looking at my viewing screen, and I see myself rocking on the rocking chair of my log cabin, where it is cooler and night is coming on, the water is turning a lovely rose."

Remember to add movement if that helps intensify your program. At my cabin, I am sitting on a rocking chair. When I want to add another layer of calm, I either rock my body as if I am in the rocking chair, or I imagine I am rocking my body. Either one helps. When in the hay loft, I always stroke the cat. Sometimes I pet the cat both in the stable and on the front porch.

When you first practice adding movement, it will help to actually move. Eventually, just thinking about doing the movement or seeing it on your screen will be sufficient. One mother picked a swimming pool as her safe place. She added movement to the exercise by turning her head as she was breathing in and out. She didn't move her arms; just moving her head was enough to help her center. Where was her screen? She couldn't create one while moving her head. So sometimes, when she felt the urge to view another place, she'd flip over, put her hands behind her head, and float in the warm water of a very calm Caribbean sea. For movement, she'd kick her feet. Her screen was a cloud overhead.

SUMMARY – STEPS TO A SELF-SOOTHING PROGRAM

Let's review the steps in creating a personal self-soothing program:

1. Select your three favorite centering exercises or meditations. If you don't already use one or two, practice Counting Your Breath, Sad to Glad, and any one of the other visualization exercises in this book until you find three you like.

2. Combine the exercises by either doing one right after the other or by picking parts of one to do with parts of another.

3. Try layering. Add enhancements. Add one from each sense. Look at a calming picture or object. Add music. Add a pleasant aroma. Remember a pleasant taste. Add movement.

4. Create a viewing screen. The viewing screen can be a cloud, a wall, reflecting pond, an actual movie or television screen. Then look at your viewing screen and see yourself in this or another safe place.

5. Enjoy, and when finished enjoying, take another calming breath and return to doing whatever you were doing.

Once you have created the right self-soothing program, the next step to making it work is practicing. Yes, that old refrain. You wouldn't expect to learn to play tennis, on type 60 words a minute, or drive a car without practicing. Don't expect to learn the art of self-soothing without practicing. Once you have the program placed on automatic pilot, you won't have to practice so regularly. I go to my safe places only when I am particularly tense and need to work out a problem. I do use my self-soothing program to help me fall asleep at night, and generally I am asleep before I count my breath more than four times.

6

Learning to Ignore Feelings

Y ou calm your body's response to negative feelings to prevent yourself from acting rashly or
inappropriately. Once calm, you must decide
what else to do. You have choices. Realizing
you have choices is an important component of
emotional fitness. Parents cannot always change
children, but parents always have choices when
it comes to managing their own feelings. When it
comes to feelings you'd rather not have, what are
the choices?

1. Ignoring the feeling

2. Expressing the feeling

3. Working to alter the conditions creating or intensifying the feeling

4. If all else fails, enduring the feeling

Feelings are signals telling you to act. Feelings help you survive dangerous situations, and when your child is in immediate danger, you want to act quickly and decisively. However, the key word here is *immediate*. If the harm is not immediate, calm down and think things over before doing anything. *Ignore all negative feelings not related to immediate danger.* This means, of course, that you know when immediate danger threatens. Nine times out of ten you do. But the tenth time can catch you by surprise. Before we talk about learning to ignore feelings, let's be sure we know how to deal with dangerous situations.

STOP DANGEROUS BEHAVIORS

Will the kid chasing the ball stop before following it into the street? She always has; is this time different? Are the kids just roughhousing or is this the beginning of a serious fight? Is your teenager serious about wishing to die, or is this just teenage angst that will fade with the next phone call from a friend?

I direct a crisis team. We are always having to define

the difference between an emergency and a crisis. Someone is on a ledge and threatening to jump; we call 911 because that is an emergency. Someone is bleeding profusely; that is an emergency. Someone has taken pills; that is an emergency. Any situation that cannot be put on hold for at least an hour because someone might be seriously injured is an emergency. All other scary and potentially dangerous situations are crisis situations. Here are examples of emergency situations a parent might face:

Toddler is running into the street.

Two-year-old is unintentionally hurting his pet hamster.

Child is playing with a real gun.

Brother is choking sister and she is turning blue.

Teen says she has taken pills.

The danger in these situations is clear and immediate. Naturally, you try to prevent emergencies from developing. You hold a toddler's hand when traffic is a problem. You teach small children how to properly hold and pet a small animal. You keep guns locked up. You keep an eye on siblings when they are fighting or roughhousing. You don't let a teenage angst progress to the point where suicide has become a possibility. Emergencies demand immediate action. All other situations can be ignored at least temporarily in order to think about what to do.

When the behavior is dangerous and harmful, my STOP plan helps establish safety. Here's what you do:

S = Say "Stop." Be forceful, loud, and commanding. Use a voice you do not normally use. For younger children, you might want to give a quick hand clap.

T = Tell what to stop.

O = Offer an alternative behavior.

P = Physically force the child to obey. Praise what you can (usually, good intentions).

Here's a quick example of a STOP plan in action. Your toddler sees a strange dog and runs toward it to pet it. You say in your most commanding voice as you walk toward your child, "Stop. Don't pet that dog. Come to me. Good boy." The unexpected use of the word "stop" generally gives you just enough time to get your child to safety. This means, of course, that you cannot use the STOP plan for everyday situations. The value of the unexpected and forceful use of the word "stop" must be preserved. So, rehearse this plan a few times to firmly implant it in your mind, but don't use it unless danger threatens.

When you don't need to use the STOP plan, the first choice to consider in handling a negative feeling is ignoring the feeling and seeing what happens. I don't mean you might not ultimately act on the message the feeling has sent. I do mean ignore the feeling as a first step in figuring out if more is needed.

HOW TO IGNORE FEELINGS NOT CONNECTED TO DANGER

Ignoring a feeling means doing nothing after you have calmed down. You try to avoid talking about the feeling. You also try to avoid thinking about the feeling. When action is required, you act on reason, not the feeling of the moment.

Some will say that trying to ignore a feeling is like trying to ignore an urge to sneeze—it can't be done. That is not true. It's not easy to do, and in some situations, probably impossible, but in many situations feelings can be ignored. Moreover, when ignored, many feelings fade away.

Ignoring a Feeling Creates Uncertainty

Because a feeling pushes you to act, deciding to ignore a feeling creates uncertainty. As Kagan points out, when contradiction exists, uncertainty grows. When a feeling signals "Act," and you decide not to act, you are contradicting the feeling's message. Add to this the fact that uncertainty is resolved by action and it is easy to understand why ignoring feelings is sometimes difficult.

Negative feelings are inevitable when you are a parent, whether or not they stem from you or your child's problems. Whatever the source of the negative feeling, focusing too strongly or responding too quickly is harm-ful. Tending a baby means constantly putting your needs aside. Teaching a child right from wrong means dealing with the child's anger in the process. Helping launch a teenager into the adult world is an uncertain business for both of you. Trying to do so in conjunction with all the other people involved in a child's life adds to the possi-bility that negative feelings will grow and intensify.

Using Distraction to Ignore Feelings

Distraction is a useful tool for helping you ignore nega-tive feelings. When you want to ignore a feeling, the first strategy is to do something unrelated to the feeling. Focus on anything but the feeling and you will find its grip on you softening. Most people can't rub their head, pat their stomach, jog, and recite a poem at the same time. I can't. (David manages all four occasionally, but he is special.)

In my workshops, one of the modules is devoted to creating lists of things to do instead of focusing on a feel-ing. Such a list often includes things that take some time, like going to a movie, getting a massage, going for a long walk, reading, and so forth. But the most important ones for parents to learn are the quick tricks. Here are ten quick distraction tricks parents have found helpful:

1. Do centering and Count Your Breath exercises.

2. Count ten things that make you happy about your child.

3. Remember how it felt to hold your child as a newborn while she was sleeping.

4. Look at what you think is your child's most beautiful feature.

5. Remember how good your child's hugs feel.

6. Remember watching your child learn to walk.

7. Remember yourself as a child.

8. Remember something loving your parents or another grown-up did for you.

9. Look at something beautiful.

10. Sing a song.

Often, just focusing on one of these things helps you ignore a feeling. Centering and remembering my children when they nestled in my arms as babies keeps negative feelings at bay for me most of the time.

Here's an exercise that I teach parents to use as a distracting tool when irritation and anger are developing. It is called Soft Face and is similar to Sad to Glad (see page 35).

Soft Face

1. Center and count your breath for five counts.

2. Instead of smiling on the fifth breath, make an Angry Face. Pull your eyebrows together, clench your teeth, scowl.

3. Take a deep centering breath and turn Angry Face into Soft Face. Think about something that fills you with delight. Smooth out your eyebrows, widen your eyes, relax your mouth, smile.

Making Soft Face when you are angry helps you ignore the anger. Concentrating on keeping Soft Face is a form of distraction.

Applying Stronger Distraction Tactics

When an event creating negative feelings goes on and on and on, stronger tools are needed to help you shift focus. Think colic and you will know what I mean. Here is what one mother told me about the feelings created by her baby's crying:

> The police actually came to the apartment. A neighbor called them. Fortunately, one of the officers had five kids of his own. He knew a case of colic when he saw it. He talked to the neighbor and she actually came and apologized the next day. I have to admit, however, that the baby's crying was making me frantic. I was afraid I could hurt him or walk out on him. I had never understood before how someone could hit a crying baby or abandon a child. Now I do, and more than the crying, those thoughts were stressing me. I couldn't stand thinking I could hit a baby.

When dealing with a crying baby, thoughts of hurting or abandoning the source of your torment are not as unusual as you think. Most of us don't act on those thoughts, but they add to our distress when trying to deal with the situation. This mother was so stressed she sought my help.

It is easier to ignore a feeling if the conditions creating it can be changed. One way to ignore a frequently recurring negative feeling is to avoid the situation creating it. It is the best form of distraction. My first suggestion was for Mom to leave the house when Colicky Kid started up. This mom was more fortunate than many because she had someone with tougher ears eager to take over the arsenic hours being created by her baby's yowls—the baby's father. (Dad was not bothered by the baby's yowls. He was bothered by his wife's distress.) But Mom didn't want to leave the house. So next I reviewed with her my rules for dealing with a crying baby.

Dealing with a Crying Baby

1. Wear ear plugs.

2. Learn lots of self-soothing exercises.

3. Don't blame the baby; she can't help it.

4. Don't blame yourself; you are doing the best you can.

5. Don't blame anyone. Well, take a few pot shots at Mom and Pop Nature.

6. Sleep whenever you can. Sleep deprivation is a recognized form of torture. Priorities at this stage of the game should be feeding yourself, feeding your baby, changing her, and sleeping. Any damage done by not attending to other "duties" can be undone once you can get back on a schedule.

7. When your baby cannot be comforted, and you have done all the things parents do to comfort babies, put her in her crib, let her cry, and go as far away from the sound of her screams as you can after making sure she is safe. Take a shower; play music.

8. Arrange time away from the baby. Hire help if you can afford it. Ask for and use all available help to set this up. Call your parents. Call your friends. Swap whatever you can swap in terms of chores; do their ironing. If they have a baby, take care of their baby one day and then have them take care of yours the next. (Every neighborhood should have a drop-in and drop-off center for parents of babies who are being pushed over the edge. Twelve hours of sleep works wonders; twenty-

four hours alone works minor miracles. If no one else can help, go to the local child welfare agency. Even temporary foster care is better than abuse.)

9. If you are being pushed toward becoming abusive, double the efforts described above. If you are alone and friendless, go to a neighborhood church or synagogue. Ask their women's group to help.

10. Don't worry that your baby will hate you, blame you, or be damaged because you can't comfort her. She won't remember. All she really needs during these first six months of life is to be kept clean, warm, fed regularly, held when fed, carried, and played with occasionally.

11. If you can't feed your baby, keep her clean and warm, and cuddle her several times a day, get professional help.

12. Figure out a slogan to help. My all-time useful one: "Now is not forever." Whatever slogan you use, put it on your refrigerator door. Read it every time you walk by the refrigerator or open the refrigerator door. (More on slogans later.)

13. Be patient. You and your baby will survive and eventually even thrive.

Just as Mom couldn't let Dad take charge of Colicky Kid, she couldn't follow my rules on her own. When you cannot do what is obvious, it's time to ask what's interfering. With this mom, shame was holding her back. She felt that if she walked out of the apartment and left Dad to take care of baby, she would be abandoning the baby. And yes, I know that doesn't make sense.

Abandonment means to forsake forever. Letting someone else care for a colicky child for a few hours or longer is not abandonment. Unfortunately, abandonment is a potent buzzword these days, and this mother took the importance of being there for her child both physically and emotionally too much to heart. She was not abandoning her child. Of course, the fact that part of her really wanted to abandon the baby didn't help: "I can't stand the guilt when the baby cries and I can't do anything, but I can't go out. I can't even put the baby down. I just sit there and cry. There is a part of me that is afraid if I leave the baby, I won't come back. What kind of mother am I?"

A good mother.

I told her about the mother of another Colicky Kid. This mother was a college friend of mine. She told me her story many years after her colicky son was grown and married. By the time her son was two weeks old, my friend realized that no matter what she did, her baby cried for three hours every afternoon. His crying so jangled her nerves that she was a wreck all the time. She was new in town and had no friends she felt she could ask for help.

Eventually, she decided the only way she could survive was to put him in his crib, take the phone off the hook, leave a note on the front door to come to the back door, and go sit in the garden:

> Walkman radios had just become popular. I bought one and spent my time in the garden listening to soothing music. I always sat at the far end of the garden. If I turned the music down, I could hear the baby, so every once in a while, I'd check. It was in the middle of the summer. The neighbors' air conditioners were working full blast; otherwise, I guess they might have worried about the crying baby. Some days I even managed to catnap.
>
> On the days I didn't go into the garden because my guilt interfered, I'd be a wreck the rest of the day. The days I spent in the garden were better all around. Eventually the baby would cry himself to sleep. Once he stopped crying, I'd go back into the house and nap until we both woke up smiling. Then we could have what the experts call quality time.

My friend never told her husband how she solved the problem of living through her baby's crying time. She knew he would disapprove. I was one of the few people she told about how she had "abandoned" her son. After telling me, she confessed, "I still feel guilty."

Ignoring Guilt or Shame

This mom's son is alive and well, happy and healthy. Her guilt is not warranted. Her guilt and its cousin, shame, hold her hostage. Under most circumstances, guilt and shame are emotions to ignore. Both are often unreasonable; however, before ignoring either guilt or shame, ask yourself these three questions.

1. Am I hurting someone physically?

2. Am I abusing someone emotionally?

3. Am I taking or destroying someone else's property?

If the answer is yes to any of these questions, the guilt or shame is justified and the behavior must stop. In most other cases, guilt or shame should be ignored. Shame should almost always be ignored; it is generally a holdover emotion. The situation might be new, but the shame always has its roots in one childhood experience or another. For example, shame is first seen in children at about the age of 18 months, often when a new baby has entered the household. Based on his studies of the development of emotions in young children, Kagan believes the angry thoughts created in small children when faced with the competition of younger brothers and sisters demands a strong counteremotion. Shame is that emotion, and it develops when the child becomes capable of hurting smaller and younger beings. Anger says "lash out," but shame says "don't you dare."

To help parents understand these feelings, Adele Farber and Elaine Mazlish, the authors of *Siblings Without Rivalry*, use an exercise in which they ask you to imagine your mate bringing home another mate because "I love you so much, I wanted someone else just like you." To make matters worse, the new mate is needy and gets much time and attention. Not a lot is left for you. The coup de grace? You are expected to share your toys and to love the new mate. This would likely make you very angry. It makes older siblings very angry when a new baby arrives.

The mother of the Colicky Kid was not doing anything shameful, however. Her thoughts were just thoughts. She was not going to abandon or hurt her child. She needed to ignore the shame and guilt she felt when trying to do what needed to be done, which was take care of herself. If you are not doing something wrong, ignore the guilt and shame and go on about your business.

The mother of the Colicky Kid needed Emotional Fitness Training before she could ignore her guilt and shame. I saw her at home during her baby's colic hours. I helped her create a strong self-soothing program. During these visits, I taught her everything I've taught you to date while Dad took care of the baby. Then I taught her to develop a good-memory file to help distract her when the baby was crying. When you need to distract yourself from a current negative feeling, it often helps to dip into your memory file and review some positive feelings.

Using a Good Memory-File to Distract
Take a minute to think about all that has been good in your life. Here are some of the memories I have collected and keep on file for use when I need them to help distract or soothe me during more difficult times:

Rolling down a hill of fresh cut grass.

My mother's hugs.

The wonderful taste of chocolate melting ever so slowly in my mouth.

Our sons sleeping.

Walking on the beach with my mother gathering sea glass along the tide line.

Swimming in the ocean with David and our sons as the setting sun turns the water pink and gold.

My list goes on and on. I'm lucky—my mother gave me the gift of cherishing and enshrining life's good moments. I have consciously worked to keep such memories alive.

I also have consciously sought to add to them every day. If you haven't gathered a similar file of good memories, start right now. Don't focus on the Academy Award memories. The big-time, starry-eyed memories are wonderful, but as you saw from my memory file, many of the things that cheer me on are best classified as small moments of wonder. When it comes to building a memory file, look for small moments of wonder, joy, awe, love, and laughter.

Why are the small moments best? They are the predictable ones. You can't win the feel-good lottery all the time. The small memories, the small moments of pleasure you can find in each day's unfolding are what get you through life's harder times. You can count on them in a way you can't count on anything else. Learn to savor these moments. Get in the habit of collecting them daily. Throughout the day, take a minute to consciously look for something of beauty and focus on that as you count your breaths. Be particularly attuned to the beauty and wonder brought you by your children. When things are not so good, you will have a habit that will help you accentuate the positive and that keeps you from focusing on the negative.

Add to your memory file any way you can. It is a matter of focus and choice. For example, I have learned to add to mine while riding the subway. I teach part-time at Columbia University, and on the days I teach, I take the subway train through the Bronx and into Manhattan. The ride takes about thirty minutes, and during it the subways is full of kids riding home from school. I love watching them, and when the occasion permits, talking or joking with them. I consciously add these moments to my memory file. (Now that my kids are grown, I capture moments of pleasure for my memory file from other people's kids.)

Second? I look for the flowers. Flowers on the subway? Sometimes, but mostly in the windows of the buildings. The No 2 train is elevated as it runs through the Bronx. I see flowers in the windows, on the fire escapes, on the roofs. When someone is rude or cross, I remember that other people take the time to grow flowers for their pleasure and mine.

A third way I add to my memory file is by watching the grown-ups. You watch the news and you think the world is full of thugs and villains. You ride the subways and you see both sides of humanity. You see the down-and-out and defeated. You see the thoughtless and the cruel. But surrounding these are the more numerous stalwarts, the hard-working, caring, striving, living, dreaming, doing, silent heros and heroines of the hard-pressed. A case in point: One day, one young man, obviously not well-off, saw and picked up a ten dollar bill that had fallen out of a woman's pocket. The woman was already halfway out the door. The young man stopped her and returned the money—an act of kindness that didn't make the headlines. The small ones never do, but they are more plentiful.

Even parents of a newborn can harvest as many good child-related memories as there are stalks of corn in Iowa when the harvest is good. The younger your child, the more wonderful memories you can collect. Be there. Collect. Enjoy once. File. Remember and enjoy again and again.

The mother of the Colicky Kid learned to call the good memories up in time of need. She learned to see her son sleeping when she needed to distract herself from his crying. She saw him in a little sleep suit her mother had given him. Sometimes he slept with his little rear end up in the air. She loved going in to check him at night and seeing him sleeping that way. She learned to center in one quick, calming breath when he was crying, go to her safe place, and flash a picture of her sleeping son. It helped her stop thinking about abandoning him. Just by the act of building her good-memory file, she realized the number of hours of good time outweighed the bad. Her son screamed for three hours every night, but he was happy and content the other 21 hours of the day. Once she learned to dip into her good-memory file, all thoughts of abandonment vanished.

Some of the parents I have worked with make a list of the nice things their children have done. A good deed list. The list goes on the refrigerator door along with the good grades and the drawings. This helps you memorize the list, and ultimately it gets stored and becomes automatic knowledge waiting to be called forth when needed. Lists are ways of building a good-memory file. So are poems or slogans or songs you can sing. Anything you memorize is part of your memory file.

CALMING SELF-TALK

The mother of the Colicky Kid was sensitive, had a strong body-mind connection, and made good use of self-soothing skills, including using her safe place and good-memory file. But learning the art of calming self-talk also helped this mom deal with her negative feelings. Calming self-talk is a useful tool when it comes to ignoring negative feelings.

The things we say to ourselves rev us up or calm us down. Stop for a minute and remember the last time your child did something you really liked. Can you remember what you told yourself?

"I'm a great parent."

"This kid is really smart. She knows what's right."

"She really listens to what I say."

"He really loves me."

Now think of the last time your child did something bad. What did you tell yourself then?

"I must be a terrible parent."

"She's bad. I've got to teach her a lesson or two."

"He's thickheaded. He just won't listen."

"She really must hate me."

Of course, when a child does something a parent likes, the parent will feel good and think good thoughts. And when the same child does something bad, the parent will feel bad and think bad thoughts. That's the way things are, right? Wrong. They don't have to be this way.

We make ourselves feel better or worse by our

thoughts, by what we tell ourselves. Much child abuse occurs because parents don't understand why children do some of the things they do. When a baby can't be comforted, parents who abuse believe the baby's crying is designed to prove the parents are bad. Or they believe the baby is mad at them and out to get them. Or they believe the baby doesn't love them. A crying baby leads these parents to think or say to themselves things like:

> *"I can't even keep a baby happy. What good am I?"*

> *"This baby is trying to tell the world what a bad parent I am."*

> *"I'm a failure as a parent and a person."*

Thinking such thoughts increases bad feelings. Imagine how much better parents feel if, while dealing with a crying baby, they say and think:

> *"Babies cry. Sometimes I can comfort my baby; sometimes she just has to cry things out."*

> *"This baby is telling the world how unhappy she is, not how bad I am."*

> *"I'm a good parent."*

Saying these kinds of things is what is meant by using calming self-talk. Well-thought-out research conducted by David Fanschel at Columbia University revealed an important difference between a parent who abuses a child and a parent who doesn't. The abuse starts in the things the parent says and thinks about what is going on. According to Fanschel's research, abusive parents taught to understand why babies cry, then taught to turn their negative self-talk into positive self-talk, stop abusing their babies. Thus learning to control your internal sound track is an important emotional fitness task.

SLOGANS

Advertising people use slogans to great advantage. You should too. Slogans keep you focused on what is positive and can drown out negative self-talk. One father of twelve-year-old twins found slogans were key to a self-soothing program that helped him stay in control. The other exercises helped, but the various slogans he fashioned for himself and practiced a hundred times a day made the difference. His problem? Homework.

His sons had been solid students until puberty set in. Kagan explains that by the third grade most kids have decided whether they are the brightest, dumber than dumb, or somewhere between these two extremes. The brightest kids generally maintain a high level of motivation throughout all their school years. The others take a junior high school siesta from book-learning and test their mettle in other areas. (Everyone wants to be the best in some area.)

This drives parents crazy. It drove this father crazy.

No matter what he did, he couldn't get his sons to buckle down and study. He ended up in one of my workshops and then saw me for some personal one-on-one help.

I generally tell parents of sixth and seventh graders to play it cool when the grades start to fall. Unless the child has a learning disability or serious emotional problem, the best tactics to employ are expressing sympathy for falling marks, remarking that school gets more difficult year by year, and asking what you can do to help. Any pressure from the parent to force the child to study generally turns a struggle between the child and the school into a fight between parent and child rather than child and his own conscience. This is really the time when psychologist and author of Parent Effectiveness Training Thomas Gordon's natural consequences works best.

Some parents can't stand the idea of letting a child's grades fall, but this dad understood the value of helping his kids become self-starters. His parents had been on his back throughout his high school years. When he went off to college and Mom and Dad weren't around to check up, he couldn't get himself to do the required work. He wished his parents had taken a backseat. While he didn't want to nag and yell as his parents had, he found it hard not to get angry when homework wasn't done and teachers complained.

We developed three slogans to help Dad stay calm and focused on his goal. One slogan he used with the teachers, one with the boys, and the final one he used for himself to help his internal peace of mind. To the teachers, Dad focused on acknowledging their concern. After listening to a teacher's complaint, Dad would say,

"I'll do my best to keep them on track. They're good kids, it's a difficult age, do your best, they'll make it." A rather long slogan, but it's what Dad felt he had to say. Memorizing it helped him stay calm. Sometimes he only said part of it, sometimes he said the whole thing three or four times when talking with a teacher about the problems his sons were presenting.

For the kids, Dad decided to say, "When it's important to you, you'll do better." For his own peace of mind, Dad used two slogans: "Live and let fail now" was one, and "Success often starts in failure" the other.

These slogans reminded him that letting his sons learn how to set priorities would serve them better than being driven to do right by their father and mother. Most kids know that the important years for grades as far as college goes are the last three years, not the sixth, seventh, and eighth grades. Moreover, most kids hate to fail or slip below their personal standard almost as much as they hate being nagged. Leave them alone and eventually they'll drag home better grades.

This father's goal of ending the angry fights was achieved. It took a year before the kids settled back down to working hard on learning, but the fight had been within themselves, not between them and their father. That was the goal. That was what was important, and the slogans helped Dad stay focused. Not all slogans need to be tailor-made; general slogans are often just as useful.

Rules for Making Slogans

The shorter and snappier the slogan, the better. In keeping with the concept of layering, I try to keep my slogans short enough to say while exhaling during a calming breath. Some people find one slogan is enough. I think it is more helpful to have lots of slogans to use. Some situations call for one slogan, other situations for another. Here are some examples:

Life is learning.

Caring works.

Let go.

Doing my best.

Doing his best.

Now is not forever.

I don't control everything.

Practice adding a slogan to your self-soothing program. When you are centering, say it to yourself every time you breathe out. Post it where you will see it often. Write it on a card and keep it in your pocket. Remember, you might need to practice a hundred or more times before using the slogan becomes automatic. If you are dealing with a difficult situation, you will want to do as the dad described above did; you will want to make a number of slogans. This dad found that writing out his slogans a hundred times helped him make them automatic. Good idea.

When I want to remember to use a slogan—for example, in a situation where stress might make me forget what I wanted to say—I will actually write the slogan on the palm of my hand. If I find my mind being overcome by stress, taking a calming breath and looking at my hand helps soothe the stress away. I often do that when appearing on a television show. What works, works.

The mother of the Colicky Kid wrote a poem to use as her slogan:

> Baby's cries build lung power.
> Loving mothers go away.
> Let Daddy rule the day.

Hokey, but it worked, and nothing else matters.

7

Goals and Missions— Knowing What's Important

When you can't easily ignore a feeling, when self-soothing and distraction don't work, you may be dealing with some of life's more complicated issues. Complicated issues create uncertainty. Knowing what is important helps reduce uncertainty and makes knowing what to do easier to figure out.

"What are you going to do about your son's behavior?"

"Nothing."

"But he is being a bully."

"He is standing up for his rights and that is important."

"But you are teaching him the strongest person wins. I thought you hated 'might makes right' thinking."

"I do, but I also want him to stand up for his rights."

"I guess 'might makes right' isn't the most important of those two beliefs then?"

"I need to think this through again."

Often right and wrong are clear. Just as often two rights collide. Teaching children about life and about doing the right thing is complicated. As a mother attending one of my workshops said: "I couldn't stand it when he had temper tantrums. I knew I shouldn't give in to them, but at the time it seemed the better thing to do. Now that he is six, we have a real problem on our hands."

Temper tantrums are good examples of how goals and mission statements can keep you on target. Tolerating a small child's temper tantrum is not easy. It creates all sorts of negative feelings in you and all other adults in the vicinity. But giving in to temper tantrums hurts kids. Moreover, as the mother above noted, the bigger the kid, the harder to deal effectively with a temper tantrum. Clear goals help reduce uncertainty. Your emotional fitness improves when your goals are clear. A mission statement that embodies your goals will help you stay focused when negative feelings mount, as they will when teaching children right from wrong.

YOUR HOPES FOR YOUR CHILDREN

Mission statements are about hopes—hopes about what you want your life to stand for; hopes about what you want to accomplish. As a parent, your mission statement is also partly about your hopes for your children. Begin thinking about your mission statement by thinking about your hopes for your children.

When asked what they hope for their child, most of the parents I speak to very quickly say, "I just want her to be happy." But is that really enough?

Imagine you are looking down from heaven at the funeral of one of your children. You hear the eulogies. One is delivered by the child's significant other. Others by the child's children. Another by a close friend. Another by a coworker. Finally, and perhaps most surprising, one by an enemy. What would you like to hear each of these people say about your child and how that child lived life?

Loved well, was well loved.

Led a Christian life.

Lived Torah.

Knew Buddha.

Graduated with honors from Harvard.

Made a mint.

Won an Olympic gold medal.

Gave more than got.

Won the Nobel Peace Prize.

Subtract and add to this list until it contains the most important things you want for your children during the course of their lives. What you want for your children reflects your core values—what you believe is important and that will lead to the "good life."

IDENTIFYING AND CONVEYING YOUR UNDERLYING BELIEFS

"To thine own self be true."

"Winning is everything."

"The one with the most toys wins."

"What will the neighbors think?"

These one-liners represent some of the beliefs people use to guide their behavior, and often also serve as templates for guiding their child's life. Not all of these beliefs are principled beliefs.

Is that important? Very. The more strongly held the belief and the more principled, the more likely the belief will hold up when life gets rough. While a prisoner in Auschwitz and Dachau, Viktor Frankl, a well-known psychiatrist and founder of the Logo School of Therapy and author of many books, came to the realization that everything could be stripped from him but one thing—the power to choose how to face what was happening. In Frankl's words: "What remains is the last Human Freedom, one that cannot be taken from you. It is the ability to choose one's attitude in a given set of circumstances."

Frankl's experiences as a prisoner led him to contemplate the difference between those prisoners who chose despair and those who somehow managed to choose hope. He came to the conclusion that a major difference between the despairing and the hopeful was the ability to find some reason to go on in the face of what was happening. Those who found a reason or mission to go on had the best chance for survival.

In *Man's Search for Meaning*, Frankl's best-known book, he makes the point that, although different for each person, the meanings and missions arising from their circumstances led to hope and the will to live. Some found meaning in revenge. Some found their meaning and resulting mission in the need to witness, to be voices for the dead, or to keep an ancestral chain alive. Others found a sustaining mission in the desire to outlive their torment and tormentors.

The important thing was to have some meaning to hold on to, some mission for going on in the face of pain. Those who survived best had a belief in service to others. In terms of the Holocaust, the need to witness for those who could not helped many survive and became a more sustaining mission than the desire to seek personal revenge. Life-affirming beliefs are pivotal to emotional fitness.

Your life, your child's emotional well-being, and perhaps physical survival depend on your principled beliefs. These beliefs are not just strongly held beliefs. Principles are fundamental truths. In his book *The Seven Habits of Highly Effective People* author Stephen Covey states that principled beliefs are natural laws that cannot be broken; if we violate them we break. He is talking about the ethical principles that have surfaced again and again across the centuries—integrity, nurturance, human worth and dignity, excellence, service.

The starting line for being a principled parent is leading a principled life. For many parents, religious beliefs form the bedrock on which they base their lives. The Ten Commandments. The Torah. The Koran. The Golden Rule. The teachings of the Great Spirit in the Sky. The sayings of the Goddess. Whether based on religion or not, a principled life is based on an ethical philosophy. The relativity of beliefs in our society creates confusion about what is important. The central confusion comes from the idea that because the moral and ethical beliefs of "good" people vary, absolutes are out; "anything goes." Not true. (If you want to know the scholarly underpinnings to what I am saying, *The Emergence of Morality in Young Children*, edited by Jerome Kagan and Sharon Lamb, published in paperback by the University of Chicago Press, is the book to read.)

Across all cultures and all religions, two common core beliefs hold true:

First core belief: Help those in need; be caring.

Second core belief: Treat others fairly.

Every major culture, religion, and philosophy in the world bases its understanding of right behavior on these two ideas. I can hear you snorting or snickering or doing whatever you do when disbelief descends. Some of my students or parents do the same when I introduce these concepts, because history and the current condition of the world seem to contradict the ideas that our core beliefs say to treat others kindly or fairly. Why? Because a third core belief held by almost all cultures too often outpowers the first two:

Third core belief: Only some people are worthy of caring and fairness. Only our group—people who look the way we do, believe as we do, are members of our family, our clan, our nation, our religion—are worthy.

This third core belief allows the beast in us to emerge and undermines the first two beliefs. The power of the third belief is most potent when survival opportunities are limited. Then the strongest can and generally do usurp the right to decide who is worthy of caring and fairness and who is not. Resisting the power of this belief is difficult but essential. Our beliefs reflect our construction of reality. We step confidently onto a wooden floor, believing it will sustain us. We hold to beliefs about who is deserving because such beliefs are the floors of our mind, our being, our explanations for all that happens. You believe Mohammed is the way to salvation. Another believes Jesus is the way. When you believe there is only one way to salvation, those who disagree with you are sources of incredible uncertainty. If one group is saved, the other may be damned. Belief-system survival can become a matter of life and death for some. Killing the opponents of your way of thinking calms fears. Think Crusades, think Inquisition, think Holocaust, think Jihad.

Frightening, but there is hope. The core beliefs of this book are based on the idea that kindness, caring, and justice for all *can* triumph.

Robert Fulghum's powerful book *All I Really Need to Know I Learned in Kindergarten* transforms the concepts of caring and justice into everyday ideas we can all understand:

> All I really need to know about how to live and what to do and how to be, I learned in kindergarten. . . . These are the things I learned: Share everything. Play fair. Don't hit people. Put things

back where you found them. Clean up your own mess. Don't take things that aren't yours. Say you're sorry when you hurt somebody. Wash your hands before you eat. Flush. Warm cookies and cold milk are good for you. Live a balanced life: learn some and think some, draw and paint and sing and dance and play and work some every day. Take a nap every afternoon. When you are out in the world, watch out for traffic, hold hands and stick together. . . . And it is still true, no matter how old you are—when you go out into the world, it is best to hold hands and stick together.

The simplest transformation of the core beliefs into a principled life, however, was put forth by the Dalai Lama when he said, "My religion is kindness." His sentiments echo the basic tenets of Confucius, the Torah, and the Golden Rule. Lives based on treating others the way you would want to be treated are principled lives.

When it comes to teaching your children, your job is to teach the simple things about kindness and justice. Go back to Fulghum's essay. He kept it simple.

Only when a child becomes an adolescent can he see that life is full of complications and difficult choices. Teach your children well when they are small; then let the world finish what you have done. Teachers, friends, and life will build on the foundation you have started. Your job is to lay the foundation; then you can let go more easily.

How Caring Are You?

When it comes to teaching children values, doing so in a loving, caring way is more important than anything else. Check out how you are doing in the caring department. Imagine another funeral. This one is yours. Your children are speaking of you. What do want you them to say?

Loving.

Even when I was wrong, she was there.

Tough, but fair.

My best friend.

Kept me laughing when times were tough.

Those are some of the things some parents would like to hear at their funeral. I want to be remembered as caring and fair. I do not want to be remembered as:

Angry.

Bitter.

Scary.

Blaming.

Scolding.

When I spoke at my mother's funeral, I recalled her lioness ways. She could be tough, at times she was abusive, but she was the lioness on the defense when danger threatened any of us. No one spoke ill of her children and got away with it. She loved us and we knew it, and that was what carried each of us through. And she could be there for each of us in many special ways.

At the funeral, I recalled that she gave us each the gift of loving life's small pleasures. She taught us all to love the first snowfall, a shooting star, a piece of sea glass, the sunset. She always knew exactly how to comfort the hurting child, how to make all children feel special. She made certain the nonbirthday child got a present. She sent surprise packages—gifts for no reason other than you were her child or her grandchild or a niece or nephew or just a child she knew. She often bought and sent to you small reminders of her love.

What do you hope your children will say about you? How will the balance add up between love and fear? If you died today, what would they remember? Work at putting a foundation of love and caring under your hopes, and you are on your way to becoming a principled parent. You are homing in on what is important. The next step is to write a mission statement.

HOW TO WRITE A MISSION STATEMENT

Knowing what you want your child to cherish and believe in is only part of the job of defining your mission as a parent. The second part involves knowing how to best get what you want.

When you have thought these things through and think you have it together, write a mission statement. A sense of mission describes a special commitment, and that is what principled parenting is all about. A mission statement serves as a tool for keeping focused on what is important as you go about the ups and downs of being a parent. A mission statement should be short. One page. It should state what is wanted as well as what you plan to do to get what you want.

Stephen R. Covey, author of the book *The Seven Habits of Highly Effective People*, explains in great detail how to write mission statements. In his book, he shared one woman's mission statement. Here are some of the things she focused on:

> I will seek to balance career and family as best I can since both are important to me.
>
> My home will be a place where I and my family, friends, and guests find joy, comfort, peace, and happiness. Still I will seek to create a clean, orderly environment, yet liveable, and comfortable. I will exercise wisdom in what we choose to eat, read, see, and do at home.
>
> I especially want to teach my children to love, to learn, and to laugh—and to work and develop their unique talents.

Wonderful. But too much for me. I couldn't live up to her standards. At the very least, keeping an orderly environment is beyond my abilities. I am of the school that takes comfort from the sign "A disorderly desk is the sign of a creative mind." I try to keep things tidy. I can't. Nor is our home always full of joy, peace, comfort, and happiness. I'd like that, but I married a passionate man with strong feelings; he married his equal, and our home at times is full of Talmudic exchanges and discourse.

I only recently wrote a personal mission statement. That doesn't mean I didn't have one, just that I had never written it down. Writing it down is useful. As a young woman, I tried to base my life on the line from the Bible—"her ways were ways of gentleness and all her paths were peace." That was what I wanted others to say about me. But that was too much. As noted above, not all my paths are peace and gentleness. I try, but not always hard enough, and my mission statement left me feeling guilty. So I eventually settled for the less idealistic "do more good than harm."

As a parent, if I had written down my mission statement, I would have written the following:

> My life's mission is to be caring and to be fair. I will endeavor to teach my children to be the same. In order to teach these truths, I will be loving and fair to my children. I will teach them how to get along with other people, how to negotiate differences. I will see that they meet and get to know people from many different places and with many different ways of being.
>
> I will teach them how to tolerate hurt and distress. I will teach them how to explain evil in

a way that does not perpetuate evil. One needs an explanation for the existence of evil if one is not going to respond to the inevitable hurts life brings without hurting back. Self-defense is acceptable. Revenge is not.

It is also my wish that my children will love learning. Toward this end I will expose them to many things. I will encourage them to try. I will remind them that there are no mistakes, only opportunities for learning. I will share with them the things I have learned and have come to love in the learning. I will teach them the concept of the beginner's mind, for an open mind is a constantly learning mind.

It is also my wish my children will love the beauty of this earth. I will take the time to share with them my love of this earth. I will take time to enjoy the beauty of this earth.

In these ways, I will hope to introduce them to a way of life I have found fulfilling.

Looking back, I see that I did most of these things. One of my sons is taking a year to see America. His rattletrap four-by-four was recently broken into and his backpack stolen. He was distressed; all of his clothes, including some expensive snowboarding clothes he had worked hard to buy, were in the backpack. When he called to report his misfortune, he called it a "valley day." "Been on peaks. Guess that had to end," he said. Then he added, "I only hope they use the clothes. Then it isn't so bad."

I had been using the idea of peaks and valleys as a slogan during the past few years as I tried to comfort him through the many ups and downs of his life. His choice of phrase meant my words had sunk in.

My mother had a slogan at which I groaned almost every time she said it. Now it guides my life. I was a shy child, and she was always encouraging me to try new things. Her slogan was "Nothing ventured, nothing gained." My mountain-man kid groaned at my slogan the same way I groaned at my mother's, but he heard. Don't get upset when your kids moan and groan as you teach your values. The part that needs to hear listens.

When you have figured out your mission statement, give it to your child's other parent. If you and your child's other parent are no longer lovers and mates, sharing mission statements is still important. The goal is to try and obtain consensus. Parents in agreement about core values up the odds the kids will adopt the same values.

Accept that you and your child's other parent will not always agree and that consistency is an ideal. Life is real, not ideal. Often one parent will discipline, the other will collude. One will venerate values the other holds in total or moderate contempt. Fortunately, most of the time you will agree as to what is most important, and that is what mission statements are all about.

How did my mission statement stack up with David's beliefs? He is more insistent that the children retain their Jewish identity than I am. I converted to Judaism. I am proud to be part of a long and rich history, proud of a religion that is compassionate and just. But in my heart, I know there are many ways to God and worry less than David about my sons straying from the Jewish path. But I was more than willing to add to our shared mission statement that we desire to teach our children to honor the value of their Jewish identity and roots, and toward this end we are observant Jews and model our convictions.

Covey says to create a family mission statement as soon as your children are old enough. He suggests revising it yearly. He also suggests keeping it posted where all can see it. Sounds wise.

HOW TO USE YOUR MISSION STATEMENT

Raising a child means dealing with many negative feelings. Keeping an eye on what is important helps you tolerate the pain of some negative feelings. One of the phrases that keeps me in focus is: "Remember my mission." A friend uses "Keep an eye on the prize." The prize is fulfilling her mission. When major troubles loom and confusions about what to do abound, review your mission statement before making a major decision.

A client was having difficulties deciding how to deal with a daughter who was involved in drugs. Several hard-line parents told her to get tough, to kick her daughter out of the house. The mother came to me for help. She had not developed a formal mission statement, so we talked about her hopes and her long-term goals. How would she feel about kicking her daughter out if it didn't work, if the daughter's habit got worse? What if she didn't kick her daughter out and the daughter died of a drug overdose?

Hard questions, but important ones. You can't control what another person does, but you can do your best to think through your choices and how you will feel in relationship to those choices. This mother ultimately decided that although she understood the Tough Love stand, in her heart she could not go that route.

So did her strategies work? Not for three scary years. During that time I coached her and helped her be supportive while not enabling. The last of those years, the daughter lived with a boyfriend. Mom called regularly, invited the pair for dinner, did the usual for holidays, and told her daughter how much she was loved. Then the daughter and the boyfriend dropped out of sight. Two months passed. Finally, the daughter called from a rehab center. Mom told me later, "She thanked me for not losing faith. She thinks my faith in her ultimately made it possible for her to leave her boyfriend and drugs in the dust."

Being a parent is a long-term investment; there are many short-term gains, but when it comes to teaching values, the results are not always immediate. There are days when the returns seem too small for the effort. That's when you need to focus on the long-term rewards. Keeping your mission statement in mind and in view helps. It helps you decide what needs doing. Sometimes you can ask the other person to change. Sometimes you can even force him to change. But remember, you always have greater control over your own behavior. Doing what you think is important and acting on those beliefs keeps your feelings under your own control. Knowing what is important also helps you dispute and further ignore negative feelings.

8

Disputing the
Beliefs Behind
Negative Feelings

S elf-soothing, calling on slogans, using good
memories, and maintaining focus on what is
important often suffice to get you through
when life with a child leads to negative feelings.
When such distractions fail, voices from your past
may be responsible for keeping the feeling alive.
Such voices make it hard to ignore or keep from
acting on negative feelings because they represent
strongly held beliefs about the self or others.

"Don't be stupid, Mom."

"What did you call me?"

"I didn't call you anything; I said don't be stupid."

"Watch it, kid."

One of my earliest memories involves a situation where I did something that was smart, but others laughed. One of my brothers called me "Stupid." I felt stupid. Throughout the rest of my life that word mingled with other negative situations and intensified them.

Feelings are hard to detach from when they are joined by negative voices, particularly those from the past. Just as calming self-talk helps you detach from negative feelings, negative voices increase their power. Most negative voices begin with parental voices, but siblings and other relatives soon chime in with their own "No," "Not now," "Watch out," "Silly," "Baby," "Crybaby," and "Stupid." Then come the teachers. Some are merely thoughtless, others cruel. "What's this?" "Not that way." "Wrong." "Think." "Wrong again." "What do you mean you don't know?" "Didn't you study?" "Can't believe you did that."

When you're small and vulnerable, such voices often sound louder, nastier, stricter, and more belittling than intended. A child hears admonishments as total pronouncements. A loud "Stop that" can be heard as "You are bad, bad, bad" or "You are stupid, stupid, stupid." These are words of shame, and while most parents don't shame intentionally, few of us reach adulthood without some shame-based memories. The memory that burned itself into my mind and made me particularly sensitive to the word "stupid" was one that took place on a day that had been a happy one.

My family had little money. Our vacations consisted of a yearly one-day excursion to one beach or another. Sometimes it was Point Pleasant, New Jersey. Other times it would be to Fenwick Island, Maryland. We left at dawn and returned after the sun had set. These are short, potent, generally wonderful memories.

On this particular trip home, we were barreling down the highway when a tire blew with a loud bang. The car jolted from side to side. One of my brothers yelled out in fear, "We're going to crash."

At the sound of his words, I threw myself back on the seat in a "relaxed" spread-eagle position, my head lolling to one side. I had heard at some point in my young life (I was six or so) that the best way to survive any fall or crash was to relax. When my father got the car under control and stopped, he turned around to see if we were all okay.

He laughed when he saw me, and asked, "Katherine, what on earth are you doing?"

"Relaxing," I replied, certain everyone would know and understand why and would also realize how smart I was.

No one did. Instead everyone in the car burst into laughter, seemingly at my expense. Moreover, one of my brothers commented caustically about my "stupidity." My face reddened, my ears burned, I wanted to fall into a hole in the ground, but I was stuck in the car for the next three hours. For the bulk of those hours, my brothers teased me. The word "stupid" was repeated a number of times.

My brothers were being brothers. My parents weren't trying to be mean and comforted me when they realized I felt shamed. This incident was life happening the way it does in most families. The fact remained, however, that I was laughed at and called stupid. Being laughed at, unless you want to be laughed at, is a source of shame, and name-calling is always damaging.

Other incidents added to the Blown Tire Trauma. I have a kind of learning disability that means I cannot learn facts by rote easily. I don't know my multiplication tables, and I couldn't do chemistry because I couldn't remember the formulas. I think well, but I don't do some of the tasks required to do well in school. Often I stood at the blackboard for what seemed like hours trying to do a problem I couldn't remember how to do. "Stupid me," I'd think. The public shaming of some uncaring teachers did not help.

I was surprised when I was admitted to college and more surprised when I didn't flunk out. Gradually, I got the idea that maybe I wasn't stupid. Still, when things didn't go well, I'd slip back to saying, "Stupid, stupid, stupid." Under stress, most people slip back to older ways of being. How does this relate to my ability to be a good parent? On to the next story.

One day I was struggling to explain to a teacher why one of my sons could not learn times tables. She was a sweet young thing. She wanted him tutored. He'd been tutored and tutored and tutored. The tutoring didn't help, added to his burden of negative feelings, and robbed him of some hours of pleasure. Some learning disabilities respond to tutoring and other forms of help, some don't. I was not going to force more tutoring on this son. He and I had decided that the calculator was the way to go and the special-ed committee had agreed, but this teacher didn't want to give up. She didn't quite say the word "stupid," but she implied I was obtuse and stubborn as well as uncaring.

Hard to believe, but true. I was a college professor, a respected professional, my husband and I had run a model home for problem kids, I had written articles, I was invited to train and speak at hospitals and schools across the nation, but this situation and this teacher's frustration with my son were too similar to my own experiences in school for me to handle well. So I lost it. I had a grown-up temper tantrum. When my anger cleared, I realized it was that old problem: If someone thought I was stupid, I bought into it, past voices interfering with the present. I decided it was time to totally do away with those old tapes. I turned to the cognitive therapists.

WEAKENING THE MONSTERS

One of the strongest fighters against the pain of negative voices are the cognitive therapists, particularly those who use Ellis's Rational Emotive Therapy (RET). When centering, slogans, and remembering your mission statement fail to help, when the negative feelings and self-talk continue to return, try some RET. Whenever I think of RET, I think of the story told to me by Gerry Wallman, a fellow therapist.

> A young man is undergoing his final initiation rites. He is taken by his master to a golden door. On the outside of the door are carved panels depicting what waits within. Each panel shows a different monster. Each monster is more frightening then the one before. Once the door is opened, the boy must cross the monster-filled cave in order to reach a door on the other side. He can only get out by moving ahead. If he stops he will die.
>
> Before the boy enters the cave, he is told to observe the door carefully, for on it he will discover all he needs to know to survive. The boy looks and looks at the door. Finally, he tells the master he is ready. The master pulls the door open, and the boy steps into the darkness, ready to face the monsters within. He emerges triumphantly a few minutes later from the door at the other end of the cave. His initiation is complete.
>
> What did the boy learn from the door? On one of its most frightening panels he read these words—"the monsters within this cave wake only to the scent of fear."

Negative self-talk wakes the monsters in your mind. Those monsters wake to the scent of any strong feeling. Fear, anger, depression, guilt, or shame are all supported by negative voices. Slogans are an effort to deaden the sound of those voices. When slogans don't work, talking back to the negative voices might. When talking back, you need to dispute the logic of past voices contaminating the present. The word "stupid" wakened the monsters of my mind. Learning to dispute and counter the voices weakened the monsters.

RET teaches you to dispute the beliefs the voices support. RET believes our evaluation of what is happening and the resulting feelings are generated or maintained by unrealistic beliefs about what life and others should be like. Negative self-talk reflects those beliefs. Most irrational thinking, according to Ellis, consists of variations on five core beliefs:

Things are awful and you can't stand it.

Other people should do what you want.

Other people should be punished for not doing what you want.

People have no core worth and can be valued only for what they do or achieve.

Life is fair.

Generally, these core beliefs underscore other thoughts. Much of the work of RET involves making people aware of the false or irrational beliefs that influence their feelings. Once identified, the logic of the voices can be disputed. Disputing involves testing the logic driving our negative self-talk and thoughts.

Checking Your Thinking for Logical Errors

When we are thinking illogically, we generally make one of the following mistakes:

We leave something out. "You never put your things away." (The kid put all his toys away three days ago.) Or, "You're never nice to your brother." (The kid gave his brother a big hug just an hour ago.)

We add something. "Don't look at me like that; I know what you are thinking." (The kid was thinking how bad she had been, not, as you assumed, how angry she was at you.) Or, "I know he's up to no good; I can feel it." (The kid is planning how to make amends for a wrongdoing.)

Even when we have the right facts, we draw the wrong conclusions. "She's failed three tests. She said she studied for three hours, but she must be lying." (The kid did study for three hours; she has a learning disability.)

We think we are right, because something feels right. "My feelings are hurt. Don't tell me she didn't mean she hated me when she told me to get out." (The kid was wrapping a surprise present.)

Some say feelings are facts and are therefore always right. This feels particularly true of the most destructive negative feelings: shame, anger, fear, sadness. In some ways, a feeling is a fact; it can be a reasonable feeling appropriate to the situation and based on indisputable facts. But it also can be a feeling based on other feelings, few facts, or misinterpretation of the facts. Feelings are like statistics; some point to a truth, others to an untruth.

Checking the Logic of Your Feelings

Ellis thinks what really matters is what we tell ourselves about the situation and how we feel about it. He and other cognitive therapists suggest these steps to see if what we feel is logical or illogical.

1. Challenge global words: Eliminate words like Always, Never, Totally. Use words like Now, Today, In This Situation, Sometimes.

2. Don't guess what someone else is thinking; ask. "You look angry; are you mad at me? Did I do something wrong?"

3. Don't rely on your feelings; ask. "I get the feeling you are angry with me; are you?"

4. Check your ideas out with someone you trust and who will help you see both sides. Almost everyone has a hard time seeing a difficult situation correctly. Good friends help you maintain objectivity. A good therapist does the same.

5. Check what you are feeling against your core beliefs. If you think you are being illogical, ask yourself these questions:

Am I expecting life to be fair?

Do I expect others to do what I want?

Am I thinking I can't take it?

Do I want to hurt someone (particularly my child) for not doing things my way?

Am I thinking another person (particularly my child) is less valuable than another who is more attractive, smarter, stronger, or more talented?

Am I thinking another person (particularly my child) is worth more because she is more attractive, smarter, stronger, more talented at something than other people?

Once you have identified which core irrational belief is driving your feeling, dispute it. Have a good talk with yourself. Remind yourself these feelings are not realistic. Learn to use self-talk to keep you on track. Anytime you start telling yourself it isn't fair, or you can't stand it, or people (including children) should do what you want, or people (including children) should be punished for not doing what you want, stop and switch self-talk channels. It was those kinds of beliefs that led me to the blowup with my son's teacher.

Instead of blowing up, I should have had a good

talk with myself. I should have thought about the core beliefs and disputed what I was saying to myself. Here are the things I should have been saying:

Belief: Life should be fair.

Dispute: "Life isn't fair. Bad things happen. Good kids get hurt. This isn't fair, it is life. Expecting life to be fair is asking for pain and disappointment."

Belief: Others should do what I want.

Dispute: "This teacher should be more sensitive. She should be more understanding of the problems some of her kids have, but she's young, she is trying to help, she obviously really cares about the kids and about my son. She isn't doing it the way I would like, but she is doing her best. She's upset because I won't do what she wants. That's life."

Belief: Others should be punished for not doing what I want.

Dispute: "Hurting others isn't right, and I'm angry because she is hurting my son. But wanting to hurt her back doesn't change things. In the long run, I just have to hold to what I think is important."

Belief: This is awful; I can't take it.

Dispute: "Too bad I can't help her see why tutoring won't help. This is just a half hour of pain, and maybe if I keep cool, she'll think about what I am saying. I can take another fifteen minutes of this. Then it's over."

Belief: Self-worth varies.

Dispute: "Just because I can't do math and now one of my kids has the same problem doesn't make us worthless or stupid. Just because this teacher doesn't agree with me about how to help my kid doesn't cancel out her value. No one person is worth more than another person when it comes to what is really important. If I don't value her for caring, I am on a destructive path."

The more you practice combating illogical beliefs, the easier and easier it gets. Eventually, your longer disputations will get shortened, and calling on a shortened version will help. I've learned to say:

"This is only half awful.

"Don't like it, can take it."

"Ah, people."

"Ah, kids."

"Not what I want this time."

"Life."

REVIEWING PAST EVENTS CREATING CURRENT HURTS

In the preceding exercise, I was using RET to dispute current pains related to past events. Another useful way to use RET is to specifically review those past events from your childhood that still burn and hurt. You felt them locked in a child's logic. RET will help you defend the child with an adult's logic. That helps ease the hurt and go beyond the pain.

Most negative memories stay alive because of unresolved uncertainties connected with shame or blame. Something doesn't feel right. Something doesn't make sense. Hurt always makes us wonder why. It's a protective device. If we know why, we can prevent another episode. Often when we are hurt or shamed, our first wondering focuses on what we might have done to cause the pain. "What did I do to deserve this?" were probably Adam's first words upon leaving the Garden of Eden. Certainly Eve must have wondered how taking one bite from one little apple justified eviction from paradise.

We blame ourselves in the hope we will eventually gain control. In our hearts we know it's easier to change ourselves than to expect others to change. Unfortunately, we often blame ourselves for things that cannot be controlled. Blaming is often an effort to beat the uncertainty of trying to control what cannot be controlled.

We need to think about uncertainty when we look at Ellis's core beliefs:

Other people should do what you want = uncertainty about power, control, worth

Other people should be punished for not doing what you want = uncertainty about all the above and about whether life is fair (searching for justice)

People have no core worth and can be valued only for what they do or achieve = uncertainty about all of the above as well as your self-worth or goodness

Life is not fair = uncertainty about whether you did something wrong, or were wrongly treated

GUIDE TO DISPUTING NEGATIVE VOICES

When troubled by negative voices, look for and dispute the illogical elements, and face the uncertainties. Rethinking, revising, and reframing history dims negative voiceovers.

1. Identify those negative self-talk voices that keep repeating.

2. Go to your safe place; use your viewing screen to replay scenes from your childhood that are connected to those scenes. Some may prefer using a journal approach.

3. See all your pain as a child. See why you took the blame. Applaud the child's strength and ability to try and figure out how to make things better by assuming responsibility.

4. Step back, look for the reasons your two parents or others did what they did. Look for hurt, fear, uncertainty. Look for rational reasons and irrational reasons. Look for how they were trying to protect you; look for needs of theirs that competed with yours. If abuse was involved, look at how sad and weak and probably sick the others were. Congratulate yourself for working to behave better than they did.

5. Dispute the ongoing pain attached to your false beliefs. Remind that little child within: "A child is supposed to act and think like a child. A child can't be other than a child. You were doing a great job being a kid."

6. Replay or rewrite the scene and have your parents or the other possessors of negative voices act better and be as you wish they were.

You may have to replay and revise scenes a number of times before the pain drains away. The important thing is not to just keep repeating the negatives. That keeps them going. Even if you haven't time to work through all the details, it helps to remind yourself, "That was then, this is now."

DISPUTING YOUR CHILD'S FEELINGS

The power of false beliefs is best seen when you look at children's beliefs.

You know you love your firstborn. He feels jealous of his younger sibling and is positive you don't love him. His feelings are real. The pain is real. But the feelings are not based on fact. His feelings are based on his personal interpretations of his feelings. In this case those feelings are misinterpretations of reality. If you let your feelings of frustration get in the way, if negative voices from your past say you aren't handling things right, or worse, if you begin to blame your child, the hurt goes on. Dispute your feelings, but when the feelings are your child's, don't dispute them.

Children see the world through a child's eyes; you can't give them grown-up vision. When a child feels pain because of an illogically based feeling, attend to the pain. How do you do that? In small and large ways.

A small way? When a son complains of feeling unloved, give him a big hug and tell him, "There is no one I love more than you. You are my very special [add something the child feels makes him special]. No one else means more to me."

A large way? When your son complains, ask him, "What would help you feel my love? I know I love you, but you don't feel I do. What would make you feel I loved you?" Be prepared to say no to unreasonable requests. "I can understand you want me to dump the baby in the garbage, but I can't do that. Is there anything else

I can do that will help you feel better?" Grant the first reasonable request.

One three-year-old asked to nurse. What did Mom do? She let him. He cuddled down for a minute or two, then came up for air and said, "Yuck, I'd rather have chocolate milk." No, I am not saying you have to nurse a three-year-old if that idea doesn't feel right to you. I couldn't have. It was right for this mom and her son. Other choices? Letting him drink some expressed breast milk, or saying, "I can see why you might think that is special, but breast milk is for the baby. What else can I do to help you feel better?"

You cannot dispute the logic of a young child's beliefs. You have to enter the world of their beliefs. A father I know who had a difficult time entering his child's world was a poet. Dad had made peace with the fact that those who read his poems often interpreted them differently than he intended. It didn't bother him. But he had decided he didn't want his child believing in ghosts and goblins, Santa Claus, or the tooth fairy. It drove him crazy when his son believed a monster lived under his bed. I asked Dad why he could help let his readers create their own logic and meaning, but not his three-year-old son. The light dawned and Dad decided to enter his child's world. Dad asked what the boy needed to feel safe. "My Power Ranger dolls hanging from the ceiling over my bed." Dad obliged, and the monster stayed safely under the bed.

The older a person, the more he or she is able to logically examine beliefs; still, in the long run, it is best not to spend a lot of time disputing the logic of most people's feelings. Unless danger is involved, it is best to attend to the feeling and not dispute how the other person defines the world. You can try compassionate dialogue, but heated discussions only strengthen the need to further defend personal beliefs.

When you can't persuade someone of the falseness of his belief, ask yourself why you think doing so is important. Also ask yourself how you can be sure the other person is wrong. Keep what the Twelve-Step people call an open mind and the Buddhists call a beginner's mind. Truth is multifaceted. Disputing false beliefs is not about convincing someone else you are right and they are wrong.

MAKING SURE WHAT YOU ARE FEELING IS WHAT SHOULD BE ACTED ON

When ignoring doesn't work, when disputing doesn't work, what next? The time may be coming to check and see if what you think you are feeling is really what you are feeling. Feelings are not always what they seem. I told you earlier not to worry too much about finding the right name for a feeling. But sometimes you need to check out the name. You need to know if what you are feeling is what you are feeling. Knowing that you are dealing with the right feeling is important; it is another way of disputing a feeling.

What you are feeling most strongly at the moment

is only part of what is going on. In order to be sure you are acting appropriately on a negative feeling, you first need to know you are acting on the most important feeling, not just the first or the most intensely felt one. This is why, with most feelings, it is best to calm down and think before acting.

Is a Physical Arousal Leading to Another Feeling?

First and easiest to think about is whether or not physical arousals are part of the mix. I know I have touched on this before; still it bears repeating: some feelings are more related to physical arousals than anything else.

If a physical arousal is the main cause or intensifier of a feeling, name the feeling for the physical condition causing it and do what needs to be done to dampen the arousal. (See page 15 for my list of physical arousals.) If you're depressed and down because all your baby does is cry and you haven't had more than three hours of sleep in a row since she was born, name the feeling for the sleep deprivation. "Lack of sleep pulling me down" is far more accurate than "Can't take this" or "Baby driving me crazy."

When physical arousal is the main part of a negative feeling, you need to take care of yourself physically. If you are tired and hungry, it is always best to take care of the fatigue and hunger before doing anything about other feelings accompanying the hunger. You might have cause to be angry or sad, but the hunger definitely will intensify any negative feeling. Don't act on feelings intensified by physical arousals.

Consider Uncertainty

I find it most helpful to follow Charles Brenner's ideas that the core emotions are fear or hurt. Remember in the Naming and Observing the Feeling exercise, I suggested you first think positive or negative; enjoy the positive and let your brain worry about naming the negative. I told you to accept whatever name came. Now I am going to suggest putting the name your brain comes up with aside and think whether what you feel involves uncertainty. Before acting on a feeling, first think about uncertainty and remember that uncertainty is named, among other things, fear, worry, anxiety, panic, and uneasiness. If uncertainty in its many forms doesn't seem right, think hurt and remember hurt comes in many forms: frustration, sorrow, depression, dejection, shame, and guilt.

My guru Kagan would prefer to see feelings named very specifically, but he would also applaud the idea of thinking about uncertainty when trying to name feelings. Kagan, in describing feelings that begin in uncertainty, ends up with names like: "Uncertainty in the face of possible task failure," or "Uncertainty when confronting an unfamiliar face."

Brenner believes the psychological basis for fear or hurt rests in what he calls the four calamities of childhood. Thinking about these calamities adds the kind of specificity needed to naming a feeling that Kagan talks about:

The Four Calamities

1. Fear we will lose an object of importance.

2. Fear we will lose love.

3. Fear we will be punished (I call this "fear that we will suffer a loss of competence, faith in our goodness, or self-esteem").

4. Fear we will be castrated (I translate this to mean the fear of being rendered powerless).

So Brenner would say anger is an effort to fight off fear or pain; guilt is the fear of punishment or the punishment (hurt) itself; and shame is a fear that others will discover our baser selves and hurt and punish us through laughter or disdain.

When observing a feeling, ask yourself: "What is there to fear?" "Where is the hurt?" Think of the mother of the Colicky Kid. She was afraid of her frustration, afraid she would walk out, afraid of being shamed. She was hurt by the belief she was a bad mother. Think of the fears Blown Tire Trauma created in me. First hurt—because others laughed. Then fear—of being laughed at combined with fear of being seen as stupid.

Think of the complicated feelings created when parents try to toilet train. Meet the Stumped by Toilet Training family. Mom was trying to solve the problem by coaxing and rewarding. Dad was using what he called "positive punishment" (a behavioral approach in which something bad happens after the unwanted behavior). Dad had carried this idea to what I thought was a ridiculous extreme by insisting that his two-and-half-year-old wash any dumped-in and smelly training pants by hand. Dad insisted he had read that this was an acceptable approach in one or another parent education book. Mom thought it totally inappropriate. However, even if sanctioned by an "expert," it wasn't positive enough punishment to produce the desired effect in this situation.

Punishments have to hurt enough to outweigh the reward of the undesirable behavior. Punishments also work only when the person being punished can change the behavior. It is quite possible in this situation that the child had not developed the muscle tone needed to control when and where he deposited his bowel movements. In that case, no punishment will succeed.

Because no progress was being made, the parents were growing more and more distressed; they ended up in my office. Each was getting angrier and angrier at the other. Kagan would say they were experiencing uncertainty due to lack of child compliance and transforming the uncertainty into anger by blaming each other. Following Brenner's ideas, I asked each of them what fear or hurt was fueling their anger.

Mom knew instantly. She feared her husband's blame, her mother-in-law's criticism, and the possibility that her son would not be trained in time to enter nursery school. But most of all, she feared that she was not a good mother.

When pushed, Dad said he wasn't afraid of anything, but he didn't like the idea that his mother seemed to think his son should be trained by now. His sister's little girl had been trained since she was eighteen months old. I heard that as a fear. Maybe sister was going to be seen as a better parent. I saw that as a hurt.

My advice: Back off from the problem. Tell Baby he wasn't ready to wear grown-up pants and put him back in diapers. Mom was relieved; Dad was unhappy. His wife and son weren't doing what he wanted; he was frustrated and thought he had every right to be. I managed to convince him Baby had become confused by the conflicting messages. He was a lawyer and about to embark on a long and difficult trial, so he decided it was in his best interests to put this issue on hold for a while anyway. I promised that after two months of letting things go back to diapers, we'd try a different positive punishment approach.

Mom agreed to get tougher if things weren't getting deposited properly by then. While waiting, Mom also wanted help relaxing around her mother-in-law. By now you can guess what I did. I taught her self-soothing skills and helped her find a good slogan. I told her about my pediatrician's old saw regarding toilet-training slackers: "No kid walks down the aisle in diapers."

Mom laughed and used this saying in creating her own slogan: "Get him to the church on time." This may sound silly, but singing her slogan to herself helped keep her calm when her mother-in-law complained or commented. She also found it very helpful to work out a personal mission statement. She felt her husband had been robbed of much of his childhood by a very pushy mother and realized she had gotten into the battle over the toilet training because of her fears her son would be robbed of his childhood in the same way. In framing her mission statement, she kept this in mind, and she used much of Fulghum's essay (see pages 121–22).

I saw Mom three times. A month after her last appointment, she called me. She had been changing her son's diaper and he had accused her of being a bad mom. When asked why, he had replied, "You make me wear diapers and I don't need them."

Mom wasn't sure what to do. Her uncertainty wasn't helped when I started laughing. The You-Can't-Win Bug had bitten yet another parent. This poor mom was doing the best she could and, in fact, was doing an excellent job, but her young son already knew America's blame-the-parent mantra. Smart kid. When I stopped laughing, I apologized and explained why. Then I suggested she take off the diaper and see what happened. I told her to call me if he messed up or in a week, whichever came first. She called me in a week. He was still clean and dry. End of problem. All the fears were resolved; all the hurts dissolved. Time and maturation solved this problem; I didn't. However, I would have been happier with the outcome if Dad had been able to examine what lay beneath his anger.

9

Blame and Displacement— Dealing with Misplaced Feelings

Why do others blame parents? The fact that our children blame us for their problems is hurtful, but understandable. The parent-blaming of professionals is not so understandable, and it has created a climate that is not healthy for children or parents.

Blaming comes naturally to children. Better to blame your parents than yourself. One of my kids fell over a soccer ball and marched angrily into the house to tell me I was a bad mother. I had given him that mean and nasty soccer ball. He was three at the time. I told him I was sorry and then went into the next room and had a good laugh. But when your child is blaming you, it is not always easy to laugh; and the older the child gets, the harder it becomes. By the time your child reaches adolescence, detaching yourself enough to laugh requires great emotional fitness, for the blame seems unending.

Fortunately, the blaming of adolescents is a stage, and the increased frequency of this blaming proves your child is progressing toward responsible adulthood. You will know your child has entered adulthood when the blaming slows down and then stops. If that doesn't happen as quickly as you wish, don't blame yourself; life with children does not always go according to plan. You may find it easier to deal with the blaming that comes your way if you understand why parents are so quickly blamed for children's difficulties.

When a grown-up sees a hurt child, the grown-up's inner self remembers his own pain when he was a child. Seeing a child get hurt almost always resonates with our past pain. That is called empathy. It keeps us humane, caring. But it also leads to a great deal of parent-bashing.

When a child is hurt and we hurt in response, we want the pain to stop. Therefore, when a child is hurting, we first ask why the parent isn't keeping the child from harm and hurt. Next, we ask why the parent isn't stopping the pain, kissing the hurt, and making it better.

But parents don't control everything. Parents cannot keep children from all hurt and parents can't make all hurts go away. We can help, but we cannot keep bad things from happening to our kids. That is reason number one why parents are blamed. The child within us expects all parents to keep all children from all hurt and that just can't be.

Reason number two for the stones of blame accumulating at parents' feet—we aren't always the best of parents. We are human and humans simply can't always be good. Parents are no exception. Most of us are lucky enough to make it into the good-enough parent category, but we do make mistakes.

Good-enough parents do the right thing more often than not. The right thing? Taking good physical care of your child, nourishing your child's self-esteem four times for every time you diminish it, and controlling the impulse to abuse. Fortunately, the majority of parents are good-enough parents. But because parents aren't perfect, when a child hurts and the search for a reason why turns to parental behavior, some flaw can always be found. So parents get blamed.

"Please, just tell me it isn't my fault," a beleaguered mother pleaded recently when her seven-year-old suddenly refused to go to school. The school psychologist believed the problem was the mother's guilt over her decision to leave an abusive husband. The husband blamed the mother for being "too soft." The child's pediatrician thought the mother seemed depressed. It turned out, however, that it was not the mother's fault. A school bully was terrorizing the little girl and threatening to kill her if she told. A smart teacher figured out what was happening when another child in the class began to ask to stay in from recess. But the mother still felt guilty because her child hadn't told her what was going on.

Before she and her daughter could go on with their

lives, this mother had to let go of her guilt; it threatened to consume her. Her guilt was pushing her to reconcile with her husband despite the fact he was abusive. With help, she stopped listening to voices of blame; she stayed in charge of her feelings.

WHEN YOUR CHILD BLAMES YOU

When a child blames you for something that is clearly not your fault, ignoring the blaming and dealing with underlying hurt or uncertainty is best. The general guidelines for handling a child's anger can help you keep the blaming from becoming a war of mutual recrimination. Here are the guidelines:

Handling a Child's Anger

1. Listen to what the child says. Don't interrupt. Don't ask questions.

2. Try to figure out the feelings, particularly the uncertainties, beneath the child's anger.

3. Imagine how you would feel or act given the child's situation.

4. Be patient. Use your centering and self-soothing skills, including, Count Your Breath, Soft Face, and a slogan.

5. Do not blame or talk back.

6. If you were wrong, apologize.

7. If you didn't do anything wrong, look for what you can agree with about the anger. "I see why you are angry" is a useful phrase; it does not mean you are agreeing but offers the child some solace and validation.

8. Remind yourself the child is doing the best she can. Children do the best they can, you do the best you can, we all do the best we can.

9. If the best someone—even a child—can do, however, means that physical harm or property damage might occur, insist on a time-out.

A more sophisticated form of blaming occurs during what I call the Gotcha Wars. A Gotcha War is any situation in which one person covers up negative feelings by engaging in behavior designed to make another person look, act, or feel bad, wrong, or crazy. If you look foolish or get more upset than the person picking the fight, you lose and the Gotcha Warrior feels better. Such tactics help people who are feeling powerless or incompetent feel more powerful.

In a well-played Gotcha War, *your* shortcomings are the ones in the spotlight. You know the other person is wrong, but there is just enough truth in what they say to make you worry about your goodness, sanity, and ability

to be in control. *Their* problems get lost in the cross fire.
One dad's story tells it all:

> My kid asked me to let him buy a keg for a party
> he was having. I said no. He's sixteen—no way
> I'm going to serve beer to underage kids. Usually
> he is a reasonable kid, but he wouldn't take no
> for an answer, and by the time the dust cleared,
> I was ready to smack him across the face. I was
> so angry, I could hardly speak. He stayed calm
> and collected and rational. He didn't get his way,
> but I felt as if I had lost. I don't understand what
> happened.

Most likely what happened is that this child needed Dad
to blow up. How else could he tell his friends "no beer
at the party"? He probably needed to convince his friends
Dad was off the wall and totally unreasonable on the
subject of beer and teenagers. He knew Dad well enough
to push the right buttons, and Dad obliged the son's need
to complain honestly about his "crazy" dad.

This is not an awful problem unless Dad ends up
feeling too crazy or guilt-ridden and handles those feelings with anger and counterattacks. Unfortunately, that
is exactly what happened. Dad let his child create uncertainty and he managed that uncertainty with anger.

You are involved in a Gotcha War when you feel
uncertainty about whether you are right or wrong, and,
when the fight is over, you still feel foolish and guilty.
When you examine the issues dispassionately, you know

you were right, but that doesn't shake the sense that somehow you are the one who is wrong.

When someone is getting angry at you and you know you are being reasonable, do two things. First, start using your self-soothing skills. Next, keep a check on your feeling temperature. If everything the other person does seems to inflame you more, if despite knowing you are right you keep feeling you are somehow wrong, think Gotcha War.

Minimal Response

How do you fight a Gotcha War? The most important tactic is to minimalize your response. This is a useful technique for dealing with anyone who is blowing steam in your direction. Whether or not you are in a Gotcha War, minimal response skills are useful skills.

Minimal response means that the first thing you do is shut your mouth and limit your reaction to "the Look." The Look comes in various sizes and shapes, but its essential message conveys bemused awareness of the other's intent to foment a Gotcha War. It is a variation of Soft Face, and serves as the nonverbal equivalent of saying, as nicely as possible: "Come on" or "Are you serious?" or "I don't believe this."

Trying to make these points verbally rarely works. Any verbal response on your part fuels the Gotcha's Warrior's verbal flamethrower. But when you are attacked for a look, you can always send a second look that implies the viewer's interpretation is the problem, thus throwing the ball back into his court. A quick shake of the head combined with a slow, quiet, slightly wide-eyed stare and the barest shrugging of your shoulders conveys the necessary idea. That could be "I don't know what you are talking about" or "You won't win that way."

With a particularly determined Gotcha Warrior, you might be pushed further. Some will ask direct questions:

> Question: "Well, are you or aren't you going to let me serve beer at the party?"
>
> The only reasonable answer: "No."
>
> Follow-up question: "Are you trying to ruin my party?"
>
> The only reasonable answer: "No."

Of course, in such situations you can simply shake your head "no." But generally, answering direct questions is polite, and politeness is very important when it comes to winning a Gotcha War. Be polite, use Soft Face and the Look, and use nonverbal responses unless asked a direct question; then make your verbal responses short and to the point. When you can give a dubious or confusing reply, do so. If the Gotcha Warrior says, "What do you mean looking at me like that?" you say, "Huh?" or "Ummh," and shrug your shoulders. This will probably lead the Gotcha Warrior into spouting off with something like, "Do you think I don't know what you're doing? I know what you're trying to do. Admit it, you just want to get my goat." You can then reply with another short word or sentence. "You think so?" might do the trick.

Or you can give another variation of the Look and wait for the next question. Alternating minimal replies with the Look generally leads your opponent to pursue one of two tactics. He will either escalate and end up looking like the crazy one (not the most desirable response, but you have to settle for what you can get in some Gotcha Wars), or, if you keep your responses calm, polite, and minimal, the other player will generally walk away, muttering angrily about parents. In either case, you win.

When Adults Blame

Sometimes the blaming created by uncertainty comes from another adult. Parents can get locked into blaming each other when things aren't going right with their child. Teachers, parent educators, therapists, and parents often get locked into Blame Games. Here's an exercise I use in my workshops to help parents dispute Blame Throwers.

Disputing Blame Exercise

Take a paper plate. This is the "plate of responsibility." Since a child has two parents (whether they live together or not), tear the paper plate in half and throw one half away. That is your child's *other* parent's share of the blame pie. Don't assume responsibility for it. Even if parents were totally responsible for all that happens to children, half of the responsibility *isn't* yours.

We know, however, it takes a village to raise a child.

Tear the remaining portion of the paper plate in half once again. This second half represents our dysfunctional society; you can't raise a child surrounded by false values and confused messages and expect the parent's values to prevail easily or consistently.

A child has a genetic endowment. You may have contributed to that, but you did not control the mix or outcome. So tear off the portion of the paper plate you think represents the genetic factors controlling your child. If your child has a major mental or physical illness—autism or asthma, for example—tear off at least half of the remaining paper plate.

You have a genetic endowment. This adds to (or subtracts from) your ability to be calm or to handle things easily. I have told you about some of my genetic endowments—difficulty organizing, high reactivity level, distractability. I have also been endowed with an upbeat mood and a high activity level. Think about your temperament and tear off the portion of the paper plate you think represents the contribution of your genetic makeup to the problem. If you suffer from any major illnesses, tear off at least a third of the remaining paper plate.

Not much left. Guilt-ridden parents often paste their share of the blame pie on the refrigerator door to keep the blame and guilt properly sized. One mother sent her husband his share of the pie. He started being more involved. Another mother used this exercise to get a difficult teacher off her back. Here's what she told me:

"My kid's teacher had really been giving me a hard time about my son's difficulties. He has a serious learning disability and suffers from asthma. He misses a lot of classes because of the asthma. She wanted him to have tutoring. I can't pay for a tutor. His father walked out two years ago and is not good about his support payments. I have a full-time job. I am doing the best I can. So I took a paper plate to school. I divided it in front of the teacher and gave her my share. I told her she could only yell at me for my part. She's on my side now. In fact, she has started writing my husband, asking him to become involved in his son's life."

The voices of blame are too loud in this land. Better than blame, we need compassionate dialogue and parents need more help. The village needs to become more nurturing.

THINKING THE OTHER PERSON FEELS WHAT YOU FEEL

Another group of feelings aren't what they seem. These are the feelings that belong to one person and end up projected onto another person instead. You assume you know what the other person is feeling and act on your assumptions. Your feelings therefore end up projected onto the other person.

I remember as a child my mother frequently assumed what she was feeling was what I was feeling. I remember very clearly an incident in which I had spent a happy day at a friend's house while my mother visited with my friend's mother. When we left, my mother said, "Well, I guess you won't want to go there again. You didn't seem to have a good time." I did have a good time, but no matter what I said my mother insisted I hadn't. It turned out *she* had been very uncomfortable. She was projecting her feelings onto me. This is not good emotional fitness. Do not do this to your child.

Good communication skills keep feelings in their place. When you are tempted to assume you know what someone else feels, do the following:

1. Summarize and tell the other person what you think is happening.

2. Ask the other person if your summary is correct.

3. If the other person does not agree with your summary, ask for clarification, resummarize, and ask if this version is correct. Repeat until the person agrees you've got their point.

4. When the other person agrees you've got their point, ask: "What do you need from me in regard to this?"

If my mother had been worried about whether or not I'd had a good time—if she'd wanted to know what I was feeling—she could have asked directly and accepted what I said, or said, "I wasn't sure you had a good time." That would have been a summary statement about what she saw and what she thought. If I'd responded by saying "I had a good time" and she still had doubts, she might say, "You looked bored some of the time, but you are telling me you had a good time." If I had nodded, then my mother should have accepted my statement. If she still wasn't certain, she could have tried one more restatement, but that would be pushing her agenda and not what I would recommend. If I had said, "I had a really awful time," my mother could have said: "You had a lousy time; what can I do to help?"

Following this sequence helps keep the right feelings with the right person. Here's what I taught one boy who lived with a super-worried mom who was always projecting her fears on to him. You can use the same techniques with your child.

Mom was afraid Kid would get hurt playing football. This is a reasonable fear. Kids get hurt playing football. At the same time, kids get hurt falling out of bed, sitting in cars, or walking down a street. Life hurts us all. To the son, the risks of getting hurt were the price he paid to play a game he loved.

Most of this mother's fears surfaced any morning the kid had a game. She never said she was afraid; she just harped on how nervous her son must be. I taught this young man body scans, self-soothing skills, and how to ignore and dispute feelings.

We also examined the possibility that this mom's worrying served to rev him up in a way that could be helpful. That's a little trick called *reframing*, in which you see the problem from a completely different angle. You can change how a picture looks by changing its frame. A large frame makes a picture look smaller while a small frame can highlight, if not enlarge, the picture's content. A red frame brings out one set of colors, a blue frame another. If Football Kid could see the arousal of Mom's anxiety serving to rev him up, he might want it to go on. But he didn't. He really just wanted her to stop.

Mom would say, "Big game today; you look nervous." I taught Football Kid to reply, "You are worried that I might be nervous." Generally, this leaves Mom with nothing to say but, "Yes." Then Kid can say, "What can I do to keep you from worrying?"

What if Mom said, "No, I think you are nervous." Then Kid could say, "When you say I am nervous, I worry you are nervous, and that makes me nervous. How can I keep you from asking me if I am nervous?"

Sounds so simple, doesn't it? But we all know that when emotions run high, what sounds simple often isn't. When reason gets hijacked by emotions, things are not simple. Moreover, Football Kid was afraid Mom would say, "Stop playing."

That's when I taught him a fourth step, designed to keep feelings with the right person. I taught him to use a "you-to-me" statement. You-to-me statements help when someone wants you to do something and you don't want to or feel you cannot. "You want me to walk on water, but I can't" is an example.

When he finally did complain, Football Kid's mom did what he feared; she said, "You can keep me from worrying by quitting the team." He said, "You want me to quit, but I don't want to. I want you to stop asking me if I am worried. How can I help you do that?"

Mom at first said, "You want me to stop worrying, but I can't." Kid was able to reply, "Try to worry silently." Mom finally suggested she'd cook breakfast, but, instead of staying at the table, she would find something else to do. The problem was solved.

When someone claims you have a feeling you don't think you are feeling, first check out if they are seeing things more clearly than you are. Do a body scan and find out what your body is telling you. See if any hints of the feeling actually exist. If not, shift gears and start getting the questioner to clarify what she is feeling.

One of the most frequent mixed messages or examples of one person projecting a feeling onto another comes with the question "Are you mad at me?" When one of my foster children asked me that question, I took it as a sign that she was either angry at me or feeling guilty about something. If I tried to hit this head-on, however, the kid often didn't agree. Instead, I said, "I'm not angry, but you think I might be." That left the question of what she was feeling up to her. Often, I didn't have to go further than that first step.

When I feel tempted to ask someone if they are angry at me, it often helps if I step back and ask myself what I am feeling. Am I hurt or afraid? I do a body scan. I observe my feelings. Am I the one who is angry?

Meet the Displacement Family

Taking a feeling from one person and projecting it onto a second person is called *displacement* by theorists and therapists. I call it "kick the dog, bite the cat" behavior:

Mom says, "My boss can get away with speaking to me like that, but not my husband." Dad says, "I can't sass my wife, but my kids better mind their mouths around me or else." Son says, "Mom and Dad won't let me get away with hitting them, but Baby Sister can't stop me from hitting her." Daughter says, "I can't beat up my brother, but I can pull the dog's ears, and when Doggie goes and bites the cat, I can laugh."

The healthiest release of feelings occurs immediately and directly. When someone steps on your toe, you say, "Ouch, you are stepping on my toe." He steps off your toe and apologizes. But sometimes it's a bully stepping on your toe, and when you say, "Ouch," he grinds down harder. You learn to be careful about saying "ouch" to bullies. Bosses can be bullies. So can parents and older siblings. Sometimes, our feelings can be the bully.

When fears of the other person's response stop us from expressing feelings directly, we hold them back and bury them. We project feelings onto a safer target because we feel it is not safe to express them to the person who is really making us angry. Fear holds us back. So buried feelings don't always stayed buried; they emerge when a safer target appears.

Blended families have to deal with lots of feelings, and often the feelings against one parent get projected onto another parent. When this happens, more often than not, one of the biological parents, stepparents, foster parents, or adoptive parents gets punished for the pain a child feels toward another parent. The parent being punished is often a safer target, sometimes because the child is more certain that parent will not reject him and sometimes because the child doesn't care so much about the target parent.

Meet one of our former foster children. Her parents divorced when she was four. Her mother had many problems and decided Hurt Child's dad would be the better parent—an act of love and sacrifice. Unfortunately, children do not feel loved by a parent who gives them to someone else to raise. But the parent who has seemingly abandoned them is not a very safe target for expressing that anger because the child fears further abandonment.

When this dad remarried, his new wife became the target of all Hurt Child's anger. This is a clear example of displacement at work. Hurt Child refused to do anything her stepmom asked or told her to do. "You're not my mom. You don't tell me what to do." Hurt Child did more than disobey and sass Stepmom. She slashed Stepmom's clothes. She stole and smashed up Stepmom's car. She poured nail polish on Stepmom's wedding pictures. And yes, this is an extreme situation, which is why Hurt Child ended up living with us for a brief period.

Hurt Child was a delight as far as we were concerned. Ultimately, she went into a group home. Her houseparents in the group home loved her a great deal. I saw her briefly several years ago. She is twenty-four now, but still blames Stepmom for all that is wrong about her life. Until her hurt and anger get directed to the right person, the festering will continue to eat her heart.

When a Child's Feelings Are Misdirected

Parents are often the brunt of a child's displaced feelings. The kid has a bad day at school and the frustration gets dumped on you. The most important thing to do when you feel unjustly attacked by a child is to not take it personally, to be kind, to punish unacceptable physical acts, and to ignore most of everything that is said. Here are the rules:

1. If you feel dumped on and unfairly treated by your child, consider displacement.

2. Calm down. Use your self-soothing and disputing skills.

3. Do not reward unacceptable behavior. Hold the child to reasonable standards.

4. Examine your behavior and accept responsibility if you have erred, but not if you haven't.

5. If it is clear where the anger belongs, share your observation.

6. Treat the displacer kindly. She is hurting.

Here are some things I have taught parents to say to deal with a child's displacement behavior:

"Sounds like your teacher gave you a hard time today. Guess you are a little angry at all grown-ups. What can I do to help?"

"Got teased a lot on the bus? You're angry at me because I make you ride the bus. I can't change that. What else will help you?"

"I understand how frustrated you are when your sister gets into your things. Yelling at me for having her makes it worse. Let's talk about how I can help you plan to keep her out of your things."

Displacement can also work the other way around. A man I will dub J.R. (for Jealousy Ruled) was a stepfather I knew. Every time he looked at his stepson, he saw his wife's former husband. The kid couldn't help looking like his dad. J.R. should have been able to deal with his uncomfortable feelings without picking on the son, but instead, he issued an ultimatum: "The kid goes or I go." J.R. went. Not a good resolution.

Displaced feelings are a major source of inappropriate feelings. How can you know you are dealing with a displaced feeling? Use the following checklist to help you sort out whether displaced feelings are a factor in current hurt, guilt, anger, or any other negative feeling.

How to Know When You Might Be Misplacing Your Feelings

You may be projecting your own feelings from one person to another more innocent one, if the person involved in your negative feelings:

1. reminds you of someone from your past who hurt you, frightened you, shamed you, infuriated you.

2. is in the same role or position as someone who has hurt you, frightened you, shamed you, infuriated you.

3. upsets you shortly after someone else upset you, but that someone was someone you couldn't tell about your upset.

4. makes you feel strongly about something and you don't know why—the look on a stranger's face, the way your child whines.

When you stop to think about a feeling, ask yourself if any of the above are influencing you. If the answer is yes, work at directing your negative feelings to the right person. Displacement hurts you and it hurts the person you displace the feeling to; the only person displacement doesn't hurt is the person who created your hurt.

A very common form of displacement among parents involves projecting onto your child anger you have accumulated and stored up toward the child's other parent. ("He not only looks like his father, but he acts like him too. When he swaggers I go ape.") This can slowly but surely become emotionally abusive.

If you know you are projecting feelings onto your child that don't belong to him or her, here are the first steps to take:

1. Remind yourself at whom you are really angry.

2. Examine your behavior, and if you have acted inappropriately, apologize, make amends, and change your ways.

3. Work through or let go of the anger at the other person.

If you cannot do these things on your own, get a professional to help you sort out who deserves your ire and animosity. Better yet, work with that professional to let go of your ire and anger. Anger is not good for your emotional fitness, and when anger that belongs to someone else is projected onto your child, it is devastating.

I helped the mother of Swaggering Boy sort out her anger, and her love for her child blossomed. He looked like his father, but he was not his father. Mother also dumped the anger and found a new zest for life. She learned to self-sooth; she learned to dispute and ignore her negative feelings, and she learned to stop directing her anger inappropriately.

10

Expressing Feelings

When you are considering expressing a feeling you cannot ignore, always take some time to think clearly about whether the feeling you *think* you feel is the one that needs expressing. Think physical arousal, think fear, think hurt, think past and future, think whose feelings, think displacement. A lot to think about? Yes. Relax. Stay calm. Thinking about these things is important, but it isn't necessary to have all the right answers, particularly if you have learned to express your feelings properly.

"I've had it. Get out of here fast or else."

(Sounds of little feet scurrying.)

"You're wrong. If you're angry, don't take it out on them."

"Look, I'm fed up. I can't keep it bottled up. If they can't take it, they'd better shape up or stay out of my way."

"Who's the grown-up, you or the kids?"

"I think you'd better get out of here too."

This is a common family scene, and a common human argument: should you express feelings or shouldn't you? Is it better to shut up and put up, or let others know in no uncertain terms what you are feeling? When it comes to some feelings, expressing them endangers your health. As Daniel Goleman points out in his book *Emotional Intelligence,* research repeatedly demonstrates that venting a strong emotion, particularly anger, often feels good, but in the long term the impact on your health is anything but good. Study after study shows that hostility eats at your heart, raises your blood pressure, and shortens your life.

President Kennedy was only half right when he said, "Don't get mad, get even." He blew it with the hostility of the last two words. The healthy response is "Don't get mad, get calm."

Directly expressing your feelings can help, but only if expressed in the right way. The right way means telling the other person exactly how you feel and getting a heal-ing response. All the books teaching you how to com-municate are trying to help you learn to speak so others will listen to your negative feelings and respond in heal-ing, helpful ways. The books become best-sellers because these are difficult tasks.

Carol Tavris, author of the book *Anger*, believes feel-ings can be released properly through direct expression when the following conditions are met:

1. The person you are angry at will listen and not retaliate.

2. The other person will agree that the degree of hurt and anger you feel is justified and will demonstrate his agreement by his reaction.

3. The other person will apologize or make amends in such a way that you feel justice has been served.

4. The other person does not undo the above by an act of revenge or by repeating the angering behavior.

How many people do you know who are emotionally fit enough to meet these conditions when confronted with someone else's criticism or anger? When your child comes at you in the heat of a strong negative feeling and starts telling you what you've done to hurt him, can you respond by actively listening and carefully attending to the hurt beneath the outcry? I can most of the time with clients, often for friends in need, less often for my family. This is not so unusual.

I used to hate it when my friends thought my mom and dad were the best parents in the world. My kids can't understand why their friends like to talk to David and me. Well, feelings run stronger when blood ties bind. Although I can respond to some of my kids' and David's negative feelings properly, often I can't. The closer and more intimate the relationship, the more difficult it is not to get tangled in inappropriately expressing or responding to feelings.

I have two friends with whom, if I am upset with them, I can discuss the upset directly and find release. They can listen and respond appropriately. But not many people take criticism well. More often than not angrily expressing feelings doesn't work.

When the urge to express a feeling strikes, think carefully. Use your self-soothing tools, use RET, and don't hold yourself or other important people in your life to unrealistic standards. We do the best we can.

However, it can help you express your own feelings effectively if you learn how to interact calmly with the person who is aggravating you. *Both* of you can benefit from learning.

GIVING FEEDBACK

The purpose of feedback is to get the other person, child or adult, to voluntarily change behavior you find upsetting. Feedback can be used once children understand the spoken word. You use feedback in situations not involving major tissue or property damage. If there's major tissue damage occurring, you already know you need to be using the STOP plan (see page 91).

My STOP plan is not feedback because with it you *tell* the person what to do and then you take action to enforce what you want to happen. Giving feedback leaves the option of responding solely in the other person's control. Use feedback only when you are reasonably sure that the person will respond or that you can live with it when they don't. Don't use feedback if you are going to be unhappy when the other person doesn't respond the way you want.

Feedback increases the odds the person will not get caught up in power issues. It is a suggestion, not a command. Because most of us like to feel we have a choice, giving feedback instead of issuing an order tilts the chances of success in your favor. The No-One-Tells-Me-What-To-Do Monster slumbers on in her cage.

When giving feedback, you are striving to be like the Irish diplomat who reportedly could tell a person to go to hell in such a way that the person looked forward to the trip. Feedback relies on the power of tact. President Lincoln said, "Tact is the ability to describe others as they see themselves."

Rules for Giving Feedback
Helpful feedback is not threatening. It isn't shouting or letting all your angry feelings explode. It isn't command-

ing, blaming, placating, or begging. Feedback is factual information about what is happening, delivered in a calm, matter-of-fact tone of voice. Helpful feedback also:

- focuses on behavior, not personality or character traits.

  Not helpful: Stupid oaf, you really know how to hurt people.

  Helpful: Katherine, you are standing on my foot.

- deals with descriptions, not judgments.

  Not helpful: Clunkhead. Two-ton Tillie. You're just out to get me.

  Helpful: Katherine, you are standing on my foot; it hurts.

- deals with specific situations.

  Not helpful: You're always getting out of control.

  Helpful: You are standing on my right foot; it really hurts a lot.

- deals with the here and now.

  Not helpful: Three months ago, you accidentally kicked me.

  Helpful: Katherine, now you are standing on my other foot.

- doesn't give advice.

    Not helpful: Katherine, take foot placement lessons.

    Helpful: Katherine, you are standing on my foot. It hurts.

- doesn't give more than can be absorbed.

    Not helpful: Katherine, you walk too fast, you stump around, you wear ugly, chunky shoes, you don't know how to dance, you need to wear a stronger deodorant, and you are standing on my foot.

    Helpful: Katherine, you are standing on my foot. It hurts.

- suggests a reasonable behavioral solution to the problem.

    Not helpful: Katherine, go shoot your feet off.

    Helpful: Katherine, I would like you to please step off my foot.

- deals with what can be changed.

    Not helpful: Katherine, besides standing on my foot, you are just too tall.

    Helpful: Katherine, please step off my foot.

If someone is really standing on your foot to the point of causing pain, you are not going to be quite so patient.

If the person is a very young child, you will most likely pick the child up and put him down somewhere else. But when dealing with children who are doing things to annoy you, it is like someone stepping on your foot *and* your last nerve.

THE CARE PLAN

You are not always going to be able to follow the feedback rules I've just outlined. When you can, great. When you can't, try the CARE plan:

C = Confront unacceptable behavior and calm down.

A = Ally with the other person.

R = Review your expectations.

E = End on a positive note.

The value of this plan lies in that it recognizes the fact that parents are people and people will not always be able to act reasonably and rationally. As a strategy, it is a softer variation of STOP; it asks for change in a slightly more forceful way than feedback and helps repair damage done by having blown your cool.

My mom's blowing her stack was not as big a problem for me as her inability to admit to having blown it and then making certain I understood exactly what she was angry about. She would blow up, and then, when the storm was over, act as if it had never happened. I developed the CARE plan when I realized that while I could not always stop myself from blowing up, I could make certain whoever I blew up at knew why and knew that my anger had to do with behavior, not my basic love for anyone involved.

For example, if someone is stepping on your foot or your last nerve, most likely your response is going to be a loud and angry screech. The CARE plan helps turn loud screeches into reasonable feedback. Use the CARE plan anytime you have to let someone else know loudly they have stepped on your feelings or your foot and need to stop. Use it with small children, medium-size children, adolescents, adults. We all have a little child within, and that child needs help dealing with both loud and small criticisms. The CARE plan helps wrap criticisms in a palatable sandwich. Here's how it works on a step-by-step basis:

Your three-year-old, in a show of temper, throws your favorite coffee mug on the floor, breaking it. The damage is done. What now?

Step one: Confront and calm down. Flipping out, as long as it doesn't involve physical harm, is okay. It catches the kid's attention and makes a vivid point. Eventually, a more rational part of you says, "Enough." You take a deep cleansing breath and practice your self-soothing exercise until you are calm.

Step two: Ally. You look at your child; you remember she is just three, and she is your child —you love her. You draw on your good-memory file, you soften your voice, you pick her up gently or turn her so she is looking at your face. You tell her you love her.

Step three: Review. You ask her if she knows what made you yell. If she tells you it was because she got angry, you say, "No, getting angry is OK; breaking something because you are angry is not."

You ask again what made you angry. If she can tell you this time, fine. If not, just tell her clearly, "Breaking the coffee mug made me angry. Don't throw things that can break or hurt other people." Then hug her and say, "Now let's clean up the mess."

Step four: End on a positive note. You thank her for helping you clean up, give her a hug, and re- mind her not to throw things when she gets angry.

Your ten-year-old brings home a note from the teacher that makes it clear he has not been doing his homework. He has been telling lies. You hit the ceiling.

Step one: Confront and calm down. In this situa- tion, it will take some time to calm down, so you suggest that Son go to his room and wait until you are seeing shades of pink instead of red. You make yourself a cup of tea and practice lots of self-soothing skills. Use this time-out to make sure you know exactly what made you angry.

Step two: Ally. When you have cooled off, invite the child to join you at the dining room table or somewhere quiet and comfortable. You connect and ally by a gesture of some sort that says, "You are my son; I love you; I am upset, but we will make it through this." You can use those exact words if you want. Remember to make Soft Face and to keep your voice quiet and calm.

Step three: Review. You ask your son if he knows why you are upset. If he tells you it is because he got poor grades, clarify what made you angry, what made you yell. "The bad grades were a problem, but the real problem was feeling you had lied to me. Trust is fragile, and you've broken it."

Then let the kid have his say. This can be a tricky time. He might say, "I didn't lie; I just didn't understand the assignments." If he convinces you he didn't lie, then you have to apologize for blowing up. If you aren't convinced he is telling the truth, you can say, "I want to believe you, but I am not certain I can."

Depending on the circumstances, you can at this point move on to the next step or continue to move back and forth between the first three steps. If this is a kid who seems to be developing a lying habit, you should not be too quick to believe. You will want to focus on the lying a bit more.

The trick is to balance confronting, allying, and reviewing. Stop this process when you feel the kid understands how upset you are and is taking you seriously.

When that happens, ask the child to decide on his or her own punishment. My kids and foster kids hated setting their own consequences, but it helped with ownership of problems. Some kids punish themselves too much. Don't let that happen. Some downplay the problem. Don't let that happen either. Go for a punishment that you can live with and that the child seems to think is fair.

Step four: End on a positive note. Assume the kid is now more motivated to do what has to be done. Tell the kid you know he wants to do the right thing and you expect he will do so from now on.

Using the CARE plan relies on using both your powerful voice of authority and your love. Both are the best tools to use when you need to do more than give feedback. If the CARE plan doesn't bring the proper result, pause and ask yourself what is going on and what do you want to do about it. When you've expressed yourself about what is bothering you, and the other person doesn't respond the way you want, you have two choices: trying indirect expression or trying stronger change tactics. First try expressing your feelings to a third party. Doing so may be sufficient.

EXPRESSING YOURSELF TO A NEUTRAL THIRD PARTY

Indirect release is a way to express yourself when expressing yourself directly doesn't work. Writing nasty letters and tearing them up is a form of indirect release. You can dance a negative feeling away, write about it, paint it, throw darts at the picture of whoever you feel is to blame for what you feel, punch a punching bag. All of these things release feelings for some people some of the time.

The best way, however, is to share your upset with a more neutral third party. The results can be more satisfying but, as with direct expression, conditions must be met:

1. The third party needs simply to listen and let you know they hear you.

2. When you have had your say, the third party needs to offer support and encouragement.

3. The party can share with you what they or other people have done in similar situations, but only after asking if you would be interested

in hearing about how someone else solved the
same problem.

4. The third party can share with you some ideas
   that will help you better understand the other
   person's motivations and behaviors, but again
   only after asking if you want to hear those
   ideas.

5. The third party must keep what you have said
   confidential, unless major safety issues are involved or you ask for more direct help from
   them.

Therapists are trained to meet these five rules. Most do.
However, a good friend is cheaper and, for most feelings,
more than adequate. I encourage parents who take my
workshops to find a "complaint partner." Once you have
a complaint partner, when a negative feeling needs expressing and you need someone to "hear your pain," call
your complaint partner. Here's how it should work:

1. Tell your complaint partner the reason for your
   call. Mine gets the point when I just let out a
   big "Grrrrrrrrrrrrrrrrrrrrrrr. Can't stand this."

2. Then for a minute you grouse and complain.
   Some days I would just say "Kids, Kids, Kids."
   Other days it might be a tirade against men or
   mothers-in-law or crying babies.

3. At the end of the minute, you take a deep cleansing breath and say, "Thank you for listening." Then you start breath counting and self-soothing.

4. Your complaint partner says something encouraging: "Rough day; the sun will shine tomorrow. You'll make it." Sometimes my complaint partner just sighs and says, "I know what you mean."

5. You both hang up and go on.

I remember going to my mother with complaints about other people. She was always able to hear me out, to be sympathetic and understanding. She was also good at helping me understand why people did what they did. But she often blew it by also getting mad and staying mad at the other person longer than I did. She wasn't neutral enough. She took my hurt personally.

My mom also had a hard time telling me directly what upset her, so she often went to third parties. They seemed to comfort her, but then often failed to abide by rule No. 5. I remember once I cut my hair really short. I looked a little like a plucked chicken. I did it because I was mad at a young man who loved me for my long hair. Our love failed and, wanting to put the love firmly behind me, I cut my hair. My mother told me she loved my new haircut. Two cousins, an aunt, my father, and both my brothers, however, felt obligated to tell me how much Mom hated what I had done to my hair.

This muddied the waters between my mom and me. The others would have done better not to have shared that information. When seeking indirect release, look for the right person and make it clear you need just to be listened to. You don't want what you are complaining about to be shared.

When seeking direct release, focus on the issues creating the negative feelings. If you want a situation to change, you need to let the people involved know. Learn the art of feedback, and that will help increase the odds that you will find relief from negative feelings that involve your children and the other people in your life.

11

Acceptance

hen you can't control a situation, when ignoring, disputing, expressing, feedback, the
CARE plan, and negotiating don't work,
what's left? Acceptance. Knowing what you
control and do not control is important. Those who
do best in life are those who see their choices, act
on their choices, and know how to comfort themselves appropriately when they cannot control painful situations. They know what they control and
how to accept what they cannot control.

"Come on, there has to be something we can do about this."

"You tell me."

"Maybe we should hire someone to kidnap him and keep him locked up until he agrees to go to school."

"Stop talking nonsense and face facts—you aren't going to control this. He got himself thrown out of military school. He won't go back to his school or any other school. He is eighteen and doesn't need our permission to leave school. He says he'll take his GED exam as soon as he is eligible. That's in six months. Meanwhile, I think we've done everything we can. He's grounded, cut off from the telephone and the car. He doesn't get any money from us. He isn't doing anything illegal or dangerous. I guess we could kick him out of the house, but I'm not willing to do that, and for all your talk, you aren't either. He is determined not to go to school and there is nothing more we can do about that."

"I can't deal with this."

"You don't have a choice."

Accepting what you cannot control is an important emotional fitness skill for everyone, but particularly for parents. Trying to control what cannot be controlled is not healthy and not only damages parents but also hurts children. Most child abuse begins in a parent's effort to control a child's behavior.

Parents contribute to many things, parents influence many things, but parents rarely control anything, and then not for long. To control is to regulate, rule, restrict, govern, dominate, overpower, master. You contribute to or influence another person's feelings, behaviors, thoughts, self-esteem, and success in life, but you do not control these things.

Remember, you do not control:

- a child's general feelings

- a child's general behavior

- a child's thoughts

- a child's self-esteem

- a child's willingness to work hard at something

The list above is helpful, but knowing specifically what you control and what you do not control isn't always easy to figure out. You have to experiment, and that creates much uncertainty. Listen to one mother describe this problem:

> My baby had colic. Everyone had a different idea about what might help. I tried them all. Herbal tea, using the washing machine to jiggle her, electronic swings. I even drank beer, which I hate, three nights in a row; someone had told me that she had cured her baby's colic because the beer

crossed into the mother's milk and calmed the baby. Well, that's how desperate I was. I'd drug my baby through my milk. As I was downing the beer for the third time, I realized how crazy I had become. I gave up trying to control her colic and accepted that it was something I'd just have to put up with.

As children grow, we often think we have more control then we do, mainly because children can be physically forced to submit to another's will. Physical force is usually harmful. The stronger the force and the greater the attempted control, the more harmful the long-term results. Some tough-love parents pride themselves on having obedient children and then find that as their children move into adolescence the levels of force needed to maintain control can slip over into abuse. As one mother described things:

My husband was a drill sergeant. He was tough and he wasn't above administering a swat or two if the kids didn't do as he commanded quickly enough. We were pretty proud of how well we had done as parents until our youngest hit fourteen and decided no one, not even Dad, was going to order him around. It took the police and the threat of a child abuse charge to convince my husband that force wasn't going to work with this kid.

In the long run force is not helpful. In fact, if the main ingredient in getting kids to obey is force, problems will arise as children begin to assert the right to do things their way. Make sure you use all your powers of influence rather than force; acceptance is built on many efforts to influence, on making certain you have tried everything reasonable. Otherwise, you have passivity, not acceptance.

So before thinking about accepting a situation, you need to make certain you have done all you can do to change the situation. You will need to endure some additional uncertainty, but this is an important step in building acceptance. How do you know when you have done all you can do? Here is a quick checklist:

1. Try intensifying your usual efforts to bring about change.

2. If what you normally do doesn't work, switch tactics. If you are a tough-love parent, try some soft-love tactics. If you are invested in understanding and communicating, get a bit tougher. Try my STOP and CARE plans.

3. While you are trying the above, read at least one book or consult one child-rearing advisor whose advice you would not ordinarily consider. Do things their way for several weeks.

4. If none of the above helps, seek advice from three neutral parties on what more you can do. If they suggest something you have not tried, try it.

If you have done all of these things, you can feel pretty sure you have done all you can do to change a given situation. The time has come to turn control over to life and work on acceptance.

ACCEPTING YOUR LIMITATIONS

Part of practicing acceptance involves accepting our own limitations—what we cannot control about ourselves as well as what we cannot control about others. David and I are good examples. We do some things right as parents and some things wrong. The things we do wrong are often very clear to us, but are also very much part of our inner beings and are not easily changed. I've noted before that we tend to be loudly passionate about things that are important to us. With one of our sons it would have been better if we had been less emotional parents. He was very responsive to small nuances; a slight frown would hit him the way a slap might hit another child. When we realized this, we tried to tone down our interactions with him, but were not always able to change ourselves in the way he needed.

I remember one family of sensitive gentle souls who adopted a baby. By the time Baby became a toddler it was clear he had a brash and bold nature. As a three-year-old he was out of control. But the parents were simply not able to become the kind of tough disciplinarians this type of child needed. The parents knew what they had to do, but they simply weren't able to do it.

What did I suggest the family do? Accept that they were never going to be able to be tough-love parents, pare the rules down to the most important, then hire other people to do the socializing and disciplining. Mom went back to work part-time to pay for her son to attend a nursery school that emphasized learning social skills and self-control. Her job also allowed the family to pay for a tough and loving mother's helper who was in charge of the boy when he was home. Today, the young man is sixteen, an honor and scholarship student at a prestigious boarding school, finishing his Eagle Scout badges, and confining his boldness to outdoor challenges such as skiing and rock climbing. An important ingredient in this story was the parents' ability to accept the things they could not change about themselves.

HOW DO YOU PRACTICE ACCEPTANCE?

To practice acceptance, you need to make sure you have exhausted efforts to change and consciously face that you cannot control this situation. Then you can move on to focusing on the "now." The now is important for two reasons: One, now is all we have. Two, we cannot predict the future. What we need to accept today may change tomorrow. Getting through now is what matters.

You begin to practice this aspect of acceptance by observing your feelings. You remember how to observe a feeling? (See page 47.) As you observe the feeling, and after you greet it, acknowledge that you are going to be meeting and greeting it for a while—that you are trying to practice acceptance.

"Hello, Frustration-because-the-baby-has-colic. I guess you and I will get to know each other quite well over the next several months." Observe what happens. Whatever happens, nod and say, "This is what is now." Observe what happens. Repeat: "This is what is now." Continue to observe and repeat, "This is what is now."

One of two things is likely to happen. You may get bored with the exercise. Then shift to observing the boredom. Boredom is a form of acceptance, so greet the boredom a few times and then end the exercise and go on with what you have to do. (Of course, if the baby is screaming in your ear as you are trying to do this, boredom is not likely to set in.)

The second response is a strong shift in your feelings from the named feeling to some other feeling. From frustration, which is a form of anger, the shift might be to intense sadness or guilt or even fear. Most likely this shift will be felt as a change in your body. The shift will range from just a small bodily sense of letting go to a larger, more intense bodily reaction of a different kind. One mother struggling to accept her four-year-old daughter's weight problem reported the following:

> It took several sessions before I really faced that she was going to struggle all her life with her weight. I was mainly angry at her and at my own mother. Then suddenly a wall came down. For years I had blamed my parents' Italian "Eat, eat"

approach for my weight problems. I had vowed not to do the same to my daughter, and all my efforts to eat properly as a model and to instill good eating and exercise habits didn't make any difference when it came to her weight. She ate good food and didn't overeat, was active, and exercised, but she is just as heavy as I was at her age. I finally realized that it isn't what she eats; it isn't what I eat—it is what our body does to what we eat. We don't have a lot of control over this part of our lives.

At first, when the truth hit me and the walls surrounding our pain really came down, I just cried. I cried for all the pain I had suffered trying to control my weight. I cried for all the pain I knew my daughter would suffer. I had to cry a number of times before the pain diminished to the point where I could say, "This is what is now" without the tears flowing.

Remember Brenner's idea that the only pure emotions are fear and pain—the fear something painful will happen and the realization it has? The shift in this mother's feelings from fear for her daughter's future well-being and the resulting anger to intense pain signaled movement toward total acceptance of what was. Anger, guilt, and anxiety block or moderate hurt and pain. Acceptance involves facing the reality and the pain.

The need to search for acceptance often involves facing a painful reality. Once you face the pain, the first response may feel overwhelming. Do not despair. Although you will ultimately be able to contain the pain, at first the hurt will generally intensify.

Acceptance also involves grieving. Barbara Tomko, a social worker, speaks of the "Dissolution of a Dream." She is referring to the dream of what might have been. Acceptance often involves grieving the loss of what might have been. Certainly this was operating in the situation involving Boy-Who-Wouldn't-Go-to-School and Girl-Who-Would-Always-Be-Heavy. The parents of Bold-and-Brazen-Adopted-Child had to mourn several losses, including the idea that they could provide all the parenting their son needed and the dream they had created of parenting a gentle child who resembled them.

The grieving process is the same as it is when you are dealing with more obvious losses. First there is denial. Then, as you accept a painful feeling, there is the loss of denial. As the denial fades, there is confusion, fear, anger, guilt, and hurt. Usually, the feelings occur in that order, but not always.

As acceptance grows, some relief will also be felt. Mostly the relief is related to the end of the uncertainty involved in trying to change something you cannot. Uncertainty is already painful. When uncertainty is related to painful events, the pain grows. We ask ourselves, "Did I do something to create this?" "Am I doing everything I can to help change things?" We lie awake nights and fight with ourselves, trying to resolve these questions, and when we finally understand that something is beyond our ability to control, there is relief, at least, from the uncertainty. Said the mother of the heavy daughter, "Once I accepted that I could not control her weight, I felt relief as well as sadness. If it wasn't within my power to control, then I didn't have to keep at her, at me, or even at my mom."

Acceptance generally ebbs and flows. Like any change process, it involves relapses and retreats to earlier ways of being. The mother described above had achieved one level of acceptance, and she never quite returned to her former state of holding herself and her daughter fully responsible for their weight problems. But she did have days when she crossed the line between trying to influence and trying to control what could not be controlled. Like any other emotional fitness skill, acceptance grows when practiced.

12

Radical Acceptance

Ultimately, with enough practice, acceptance can be strengthened to a point where it can become a powerful antidote to pain and trauma. Marsha Linehan speaks of *radical* a*cceptance*. She says it is the only way out of hell. The "hell" she refers to is the one created by traumatic experiences. Becoming a parent is a joyous as well as a difficult experience. The joy and pleasure usually outweigh the difficulty and pain, so we do not think of parenting as trauma-filled. But often it is. Radical acceptance is the key to survival when trauma visits you or your child.

As we struggle to accept a pain that is not easily put aside, we almost always ask, "Why?" Sometimes it is "Why me?" Sometimes it is "Why my child?" Whatever answer we come to ultimately forms part of the equation that determines how we go on with our lives and whether or not we are emotionally fit.

"Why this?"

"Maybe it's God's punishment."

"To hurt an innocent child?"

"The Bible says the sins of the father are visited on the children for seven generations."

"I can't accept that."

I once heard Linehan use the following story in an effort to help the audience understand when the time had come to think about the need for radical acceptance. She asked us to imagine that an earthquake had struck our home and our house had fallen down around us. It was night and all the lights were out. Our child was crying in the darkness. We called out to him to come to where we were but he just cried louder. We renewed our efforts to get him to come to us as we tried also to go to him. We were doing what we could, but he did not seem to be making any effort. We began to add anger to our efforts to get him to move toward us. Ultimately, we reached his room, only to find the way blocked by debris except for one hole big enough for him but not for us to climb through. All he needed to do was crawl a few feet and grab our hands. We'd do the rest. Suddenly the building shook with an aftershock. Fearful and frustrated, we began to yell at our beloved son to come to us or else. Then dawn broke, and we could see our son. He was trapped by a fallen timber and could not move. The time had come to accept that this pain-filled situation was out of our hands. Linehan's radical acceptance involves facing the worst life offers us and going on . . .

The earthquake-trapped parent described by Linehan had every right to ask, "Why me?" "Why my child?" But such questions would have wasted the precious time left. Asking why interferes with acceptance and doing what can be done to endure, get through, and go on.

Our mission statements explore our hopes and goals. In creating them we had to look at some of our core beliefs. When we examined the irrationality of some of our thoughts we were also examining our core beliefs. Radical acceptance demands another look at core beliefs, but at the ones that serve as explanations for tragic and traumatic events. Without such explanations, life ultimately defeats us. We give up, blame ourselves, blame others, turn away from good, or seek revenge.

The quest for revenge begins when the quest for love and connection to others fails—then the power of striking back assumes disproportionate control. Hurt and trauma almost always turn us to thoughts of revenge—wanting to strike back, to hurt someone who has hurt us is part of our fight-or-flight response. As such it is programmed into our genes and therefore often feels right and natural; fighting when attacked kept us alive when wild animals stalked the night. But it is an outdated response. Until we learn to go beyond hurt and reach for a higher way of being, however, we will not find peace in our hearts or on earth, particularly in times of trauma.

This is not an impossible task, for while many believe we are more prone to violence than to good deeds, the facts seem to show otherwise. For example, being abused is a traumatic and painful experience, but not all battered and abused children grow up to batter and abuse their own children. The statistics show that only thirty percent of those who are abused become abusers.

My mother had been physically abused. Some days she was tied up and left for hours in the woods by an older sister charged with taking her to the beach for the day. The sister didn't want her little sister tagging along. This same sister beat my mother and threatened to kill her if she told anyone about being tied up or about the beatings. Even after all this, my mother did not beat her children. She did not tie them up and leave them. She was in no way physically abusive. Moreover, my mother, as the statistics above suggest, represents a norm.

I believe we were created to be caring; when we are not, something has gone terribly wrong with our lives. One of the things that sometimes goes wrong is the inability of our core beliefs to hold up against life's realities. The more attuned those beliefs are with reality, the more likely you will stay emotionally fit in the face of hurt and pain.

Robert Coles, a Harvard psychiatrist noted for his

studies of children, discovered that many who survived lives of pain did so because their parents instilled in them a sustaining religious faith. One of his most moving stories is about Ruby Bridges.

Ruby was one of the children attempting to integrate the previously all-white schools of the South. She was six years old and in the first grade. Daily, she was marched into her school—a small child walking a gauntlet of hatred. The crowd screamed obscenities, threatened violence, spat at her. One day Coles saw her pause and look out over the crowd. Her lips moved. He wondered what she was saying to the crowd. Coles later asked Ruby what she said.

"I wasn't talking to them," she told him. "I had forgotten to pray for them, so I had to stop and ask God to forgive them. That was what our Lord did when they nailed Him to the cross." This story appears in Coles's book *The Spiritual Life of Children*.

The faith of children is simple and effective. Part of its effectiveness stems from the fact that they don't question; they have a protective shell that allows them to accept what is, what parents tell them about why suffering exists. Ruby believed those who hated and reviled her had not felt God's love and therefore needed her prayers. She believed if they knew God's love, they would not do what they were doing. She believed her mission was to pray for them and to forgive them.

Some of us keep a child's faith no matter what life brings us. If you are one whose faith never quails or quakes, you have been truly blessed. If you do not have a sustaining faith of some sort, now is the time to develop one. Your emotional fitness depends on a having some sustaining belief that will carry you through times of serious trouble.

James Garbarino, an expert on trauma, says traumatic life blows often destroy our protective shells. Most of us like to think the world is safe—that we are safe, our children are safe, and, because most people are good people, that reason will prevail, and we will stay safe. These are what Garbarino refers to as protective shells surrounding secrets we do not want revealed to us or our children.

Children believe that what is, is everywhere and for all time. If children are safe and well cared for, they believe they will always be safe and well cared for. The first protective shell that trauma destroys is this idea. Trauma reminds us all we are fragile, that injury and illness cannot always be avoided, and that death is inevitable. Garbarino calls the unveiling of this bit of hidden knowledge Snowdon's Secret.

Snowdon was the bombardier in the plane flown by Yossarian, the hero in Joseph Heller's *Catch-22*. After returning from a mission in which their plane is hit, Yossarian pulls an unconscious Snowdon from the plane. Snowdon initially appears to be only slightly wounded, but when Yossarian opens the bombardier's leather jacket he discovers blood, guts, gore. Yossarian learns what we prefer to keep from conscious knowledge: despite appearances, the human body is frail and easily destroyed. We are ultimately powerless; we cannot defeat death.

Another protective shell that trauma destroys is called Dantrell Davis's Secret by Garbarino. It relates to our powerlessness in the face of human irrationality. Dantrell Davis was a seven-year-old African-American youngster. He lived in a rough section of Chicago. His mother had walked him to school. When they were about 75 feet from the school door, where Dantrell's teacher was waiting, Dantrell left his mother's side and ran toward the school. Before he reached the school's door he was dead, shot in the head by a sniper. Two policemen were standing less than 150 feet away. Dantrell's Secret: the unthinkable, the irrational cannot be stopped even when your mother is by your side and the police are standing on the corner.

Garbarino calls the third secret Milgrim's Secret. This secret reveals the weakness of our good selves and our vulnerability to those in power. Milgrim was the psychologist who induced perfectly nice and upstanding citizens to inflict what they thought were painful and life-threatening shocks for the sake of helping with a scientific experiment. Milgrim's Secret teaches us that given the right circumstances we can all set aside our good selves and turn violent. Caring people can be made immune to others' pain. Good people do bad things.

Part of being emotionally fit involves the ability to accept pain without turning against life. We need reasonable explanations for why bad things happen and why good people do bad things in order to achieve Radical Acceptance.

EXAMINING YOUR BELIEFS
ABOUT WHY BAD THINGS
HAPPEN

When I am teaching parents to examine these issues in a workshop, I use an exercise I call Why You Think Bad Things Happen. It begins by making a life-line. Take a blank sheet of paper and draw a line down the middle, beginning about an inch from the top and ending an inch from the bottom. At the top of the line put today's date and at the bottom your birth date. You will fill it in more in a moment.

First, take a few minutes to center. Go to your safe place and put up your viewing screen. Ask the screen to reveal the earliest memory you have of something painful that happened to you and that made you think about why bad things happen. Some people can't remember anything about their life until their teens. If that is you, don't worry; just go for the first painful memory you can recall. It need not be a memory others would think was traumatic—one person's definition of an extremely painful situation may be another's definition of a minor annoyance. You are looking for the events from your life that hurt you and shaped your ideas about why bad things happen.

Some have cited the birth of siblings, others sexual abuse, and still others feeling betrayed by their parents when they discovered Santa Claus was not an actual person. No matter the size of the hurt involved in your first painful memory, give it a name and write that name near the bottom of the page of your life-line. Continue to examine your life, and note and name in chronological order the various pains you have endured. Stop when you have five memories.

Now examine each painful memory for the beliefs it led you to hold. Those beliefs may or may not be similar to the ones we have already talked about. The important thing is to look at what these experiences meant to you and what conclusions you drew from them.

The next step in the exercise is to look at the positives that came from the memories and the beliefs. Some believe painful events are lessons. I don't think the purpose of painful experiences is to teach lessons any more than I think they are punishments. I do think lessons are there for the learning, however, but only if we look for them. So look for the lessons, particularly those that added to your ability to stay focused on what was important to you in life. One of the purposes of this exercise is to look for positive lessons. For each painful memory you should be able to note at least one positive outcome.

The next step involves using the memories to examine your feelings about why people hurt people. Most of the hurts identified in the first part of this chapter are inflicted by other people. While sometimes the pain comes from natural disasters, illness, or true accidents, the majority of the memories reported by people involve hurt inflicted by others. As Kagan notes, other people are a source of uncertainty. When the uncertainty ends in a painful certainty involving another person, the relationship becomes strained. The strains can be best dealt with when you have reasonable explanation for why people do hurtful things.

To complete this part of the exercise, list five to ten reasons people harm other people. Some people find it most helpful to find one specific reason per memory and then expand from there.

The final step in the exercise asks you to write a one-page explanation for life's inevitable suffering. Doing this exercise makes some people accuse me of teaching philosophy or of preaching. But I am not invested in teaching a specific religion or philosophy; I am interested in having you and other parents understand the importance of having core beliefs that help you explain and make sense of the world. I also don't think you are emotionally fit if those beliefs are not life-affirming, do not take a caring attitude toward others, or are not founded on justice for all.

Here is a sample of the way one parent did this exercise:

The first painful memory: My sister's birth.

The beliefs: That I wasn't the center of the universe. That my parents hadn't been pleased with me or they wouldn't have had another baby. That because I wanted to hurt the baby, I was bad. If I didn't stop being bad, my parents might give me away.

The positive: Learning to control my anger. I wanted to kill my sister, but I learned to take those feelings and put them aside. Eventually, my sister and I became good friends, although I think that took until we were in our teens.

The why: Now I see that my parents enjoyed being parents; they didn't want me to be an only child. In fact, my father was an only child and felt it had limited him in many ways.

Another painful memory: My best friend eloping with my boyfriend. They ended up married, but it didn't last. They both cheated on each other.

The beliefs: You can't really trust anyone. You are on your own.

The positive. Learning I could live without both of them and that I could survive betrayal. Another positive was I became more independent, less dependent on others. I became more realistic about what I expected from others. I have a better marriage than most of my friends because of that.

The why: Obviously, they "loved" each other more than they loved me. That certainly changed my beliefs about love. I think what they felt was lust. I also realized that I hadn't taken enough care of me. I had such blind faith in both of them that I encouraged them to spend time alone together. I hate tennis, they both loved the game, and that is when their romance blossomed.

A third painful memory: My Uncle Chris's death. He was only forty-five and died unexpectedly.

The beliefs: Life really isn't fair. He was the best of people. He had just reached the point where he was accomplishing some good and doing the things he believed in when he died.

The positive: Can't think of one. It still just hurts. He was special to me and I never told him. I won't do that again, and maybe that is the upside. It isn't much, considering the loss; his death shook my faith. When the priest started talking about heaven and God's will, I almost had to leave the church.

The why: Why do good people die? Why does anyone die? Maybe this life is just a passage to a better life. My mother believes the good die young because God wants them to come to His side. If I could believe that I would find it comforting, but I'm not certain. A friend of mine believes in reincarnation. I can't believe that either. I know you can't have life without death, but that isn't very comforting.

And she went on to write and think about each succeeding painful memory as her life had progressed. Here's what she wrote about why bad things happen:

I don't know anymore. I think it is something like the bumper sticker says—S– – – Happens. As I little girl, I loved the idea that God ordered everything. I figured when something bad happened, it was a punishment. I could always figure out what I or the other person had done wrong. Now I no longer go to church and I realize that isn't good, but I also don't believe the things the priest says anymore.

It is easier to figure out why people hurt other people. Sometimes it is just ignorance, not knowing better, or not stopping to think. Most of the hurts my parents inflicted on me were of that kind. Then there is thinking you have to have something and someone else thinking they have to have it too. Works okay when it is something you can both have, but lots of times you can't both have it. I think the best example of this is the abortion issue. The baby has a right to life and so does the mother.

I still believe in trying to be a good person. It just makes more sense and feels better than being a bad person.

No matter what the painful memories people end up describing, the beliefs are almost always variations in one way or another on Garbarino's secrets or Ellis's irrational beliefs.

I asked an atheist friend of mine what beliefs sustained her. She believes this world is all we have. That no creator exists. That no force works in our lives but our own efforts. Given that, we can work for good or evil. She finds comfort in working for good. When life blows come and destroy or take away all that we love, we can give up or go on. If we give up, we lose, so she doesn't give up. Life is short, and for all its hurt and pain, also has moments of joy and pleasure. Joy alternates with pain, and since that is all we have, we go on.

Whatever beliefs you have come to, hope lies in focusing on those that sustain a connection to what is good. Life's inevitable blows can destroy or take away all that we love. The temptation is to give up trying to stay connected to the power of what is good. If we give up on our connections to one another we lose. We need our connections to others. We need to work for good. When we have suffered, there is healing in helping others. In the long run, our connections to each other are all that sustain. That is why we have children; that is why we help one another.

Honoring Your Strength Exercise

Do a quick "brainstorming" and make a list of all you have survived. Write every hurt and slight, bump and bruise, tragedy and trauma you can recall in fifteen minutes to half an hour. Do not dwell on them; just write them down, by name or by a quick phrase that says it all to you.

When you are done, read it again. After each event, remind yourself, "I got past that. I'm still going. That didn't defeat me." Whatever trauma, whatever hurtful changes life has dealt you, you have survived and you are strong. I know you are because you are still trying. You are reading this book; you are trying to do better.

Here is a final meditation that honors your strength. This is an exercise you can teach your children as well:

Plant your feet solidly on the floor.

Sit tall and strong.

Place your hands on your thighs.

Keep your eyes open but focused on a spot on the wall.

Breathe in and, as you do, press your feet into the floor more and press your hands down. Feel the strength build. When you have gathered it, hold it for a few seconds, and as you breathe out, release and relax. Strength training involves releasing and relaxing as well as gathering strength.

Notice the difference in feeling between gathering and holding, releasing and relaxing. Take another breath, gather your strength, hold it, and then breathe out and rest. As you rest, breathe normally and smile the smile of the victor. The victor's smile is a smile of satisfaction. A half smile. Notice how that feels. This is the power meditation routine.

Figure out a cycle that works best for you. Some gather and hold their strength and then release it and smile every fourth breath. Others simply do it every time they find they want to, and still others anytime their mind has wandered. Do whatever works for you. Remember, however, to smile the smile of the victor in honor of your strength. As you do the exercise, notice how good it feels to gather your strength, to notice it, and then to rest it. As you end it, express your gratitude for the good in your life. When you are done with the exercise, stretch and smile and go on.

This life is hard, but we can go forward toward love and all that is good in this world. If we keep ourselves turned toward what is good, we can keep the world moving toward the good also.

13

Living
Emotional
Fitness

"See the beautiful yunyet."

I was three when I first called my parents and brothers to come and "See the beautiful yunyet." I was echoing my mother's words. Few days went by in our family without her calling us to look out the window, sit on the porch, or walk out into the yard so we could watch day fade into night. I couldn't pronounce the words, but an emotional fitness exercise had been built into my being and it continues to comfort me. Do something every day at the same time and in the same way for enough days in a row and ultimately you will do it automatically. That is why throughout the book I have asked you again and again to practice, practice, practice.

Taking time to enjoy and honor what is good is an emotional fitness exercise. Earlier in this book, I stated that most people sit up naturally, but that doing sit-ups properly requires a more conscious effort. My mother taught me to love nature. I do it naturally. It becomes an emotional fitness exercise when I do it consciously and with awareness. That is why I ask you to center before and after each exercise. It enhances the benefits. Some call this "living in the now," others call it becoming one with what you do, and still others refer to it as mindfulness.

The name doesn't matter, but centering yourself and focusing fully on what you are doing turns a naturally occurring happening into something stronger. Developing an emotional fitness program also enhances the power of the individual exercises. Most people take some time to enjoy something of beauty regularly, but many never use that moment to also take the time to be with something beautiful in a way that improves their emotional fitness.

A formal program helps in another way. Just as the best physical fitness programs involve cross-training and full-body workouts, the best emotional fitness training program develops all the major emotional fitness skills. What follows is a total Emotional Fitness Training® program.

HOW TO PRACTICE
EMOTIONAL FITNESS

Although I generally suggest following the exercises as presented, every self-soothing program needs to be tailored individually, and so does every Emotional Fitness Training program, so feel free to experiment and use these exercises in a way that is just right for you. I suggest first trying them in the order presented for several weeks and then experimenting with other possibilities.

Start each exercise by centering. Here's a quick review. Take a deep breath and hold it until you feel tense. Then release the breath and breathe normally, counting your breaths and smiling at the end of four of them. Center at the beginning of each exercise and again when the exercise itself is over.

The First Exercise: Be grateful for all that you have been given

This is where your memory book comes in to play, for in the rush and turmoil of every day, we often forget to take time to measure what is good about our lives. The bad forces itself on us and can block our view of the good. This exercise reminds us to look into our memory book and be grateful for what we have been given.

Practice this exercise in the morning as soon as you wake up and before you get out of bed. Center and then take a minute to pull some positives from your file of good memories. As a parent, it helps to focus on the wonderful miracle brought to all by our children. And yes, I know children also bring stress and mess, but don't start your day thinking about the stress and mess. Think about the good. Next, think about what is good in you; honor your strength. Also honor those you love in addition to your children. Finally, honor what is good in this world.

To intensify this exercise, place by your bed symbols that recall living examples from your memory book. A picture of your children as babies, a seashell, a feather, a piece of sea glass, a present your kids gave you, a rock from a mountain you climbed—any object that helps you remember a time of joy or awe, love or victory. Look at this memento; remember the good.

Exercise Two: Remember your mission

Just as we forget to honor what is good about our lives, those we love, and the world we live in, so we often forget what is important and what we want our life to stand for. When you have finished the first exercise and before you start the day, remind yourself of your mission. Some people keep a copy of their mission statement by their bed. Some have it framed where it can be read easily. At a minimum, repeat your mission statement to yourself. Consciously remembering your mission will help you move toward fulfilling it.

Exercise Three: Be with something of beauty created by you or another person

This is a variation of building your good-memory file, since sometimes all you can do is use your existing good-memory file. You recall a song, a painting, words of inspiration. It is best, however, to create something of beauty. So sing, hum, or whistle your favorite song. Spend a minute adding to a poem you are writing or working on something else creative, whether it is gourmet cooking or a carpentry project. Two or three minutes early in the day adding to something you are creating is satisfying. We are a creative species, and each and every one of us is capable of creating something beautiful. Do it, and when time presses and you cannot be creative, at least take a minute to remember the times you were.

I like to do this exercise while getting ready to start the day. I find singing "Amazing Grace" in the shower or in the car on the way to work lifts my mood. (It wouldn't lift the mood of anyone else who could hear, which is why I do it when alone.) Singing "Amazing Grace" always makes me feel better. Others have told me this exercise works better for them in the evening, when they can set aside some time to be creative.

Exercise Four: Accept what is
You have been taught how to accept what is. Here is a quick review: Center. After centering, do a quick body scan and then observe your feelings. Watch what is happening in your body and your mind. Then step back and observe. Say, "Hello, What Is Now." See what happens. Smile and see what happens. Glare and see what happens. Finally, just watch and see what happens.

When you are tired of watching, or when a few minutes have passed, stop and say again, "Hello, What Is Now." Now is always changing. Accept again. When you are bored watching what is, go on to something else.

Do this one as you get ready for lunch.

Exercise Five: Do something caring; expect nothing in return

I've talked about the importance of being caring over and over again. No act of caring goes unrewarded. This exercise adds to the importance of caring—the reminder that when we give in hope of gain, we are not giving but bartering. Caring is its own reward. When you give a hug, you get a hug.

An act of caring can be as simple as giving the next person you see a heartfelt compliment. For an at-home parent, the caring can be giving your child a big just-because-I-love-you hug. When? Plan while eating lunch. When the time comes, enjoy the act of caring, not what you want in return.

Exercise Six: Connect, if only in your heart or memory, with someone who nourishes your inner being

This exercise narrows using your memory book to recalling people who nurtured you. I've pointed out over and over again the importance of honoring those who have nourished us. We too quickly recall past hurts. Recalling the good we have been given is healthier. This exercise asks you to spend a minute, honoring someone from your past who has nourished you. A remembered act of caring nourishes eternally, providing you remember it. Remember an act of love by a mother, father, sister, brother, grandparent, teacher, friend. Recall the act and the person. Enjoy and be nourished yet again.

Practice this as the afternoon is drawing to an end.

Exercise Seven: Do something that yields a quick and concrete result

This particular exercise has not been discussed before, at least directly. It has been alluded to when the concept of distracting was looked at. Doing something concrete can help distract you from negative feelings. Here the exercise serves a slightly different purpose.

We are often disconnected from the fruits of our labor. We can't see the value of what we are doing. For some, paychecks are often the only concrete measurement of work done; for others it might be a grade or a report card. Sometimes the full results of our work will not be visible for many years. This is not good for our being. Doing something, no matter how small, that yields an immediate concrete and positive result is good for our souls and our well-being. For me folding laundry is such a task. It relaxes me. On frustrating days folding a basket of laundry makes me feel I've at least done one thing of value. Write a postcard to a friend, clean a drawer, chop some wood, tend a flowerpot.

Some find it useful to spend a minute or two at the end of their regular workday making certain they have done something concrete that they can take pleasure in before calling it a day. Others like to do it after dinner.

Exercise Eight: Do something just for you
The day is empty that does not hold something that is pure pleasure just for you. Doing something for you is the gift you give to yourself. And it helps you keep giving to others. Taking conscious pleasure in this just-for-you activity is important. Moreover, it must never be a "should." Some people exercise and see that as what they do just for themselves, but they don't enjoy it and have to push themselves to do it. So if this is you, keep on exercising, but find something you need no urging to do and that is just for you. I read what I want to read, not what I have to read, for at least fifteen minutes before turning out my light at night. That is one of my just-for-me pleasures. Some days letting a chocolate Kiss melt in my mouth is my just-for-me pleasure.

Exercise Nine: Let go of a negative; hold on to a positive
This exercise builds acceptance. Do it before you go to sleep. (Some like to do it over a cup of herbal tea or hot chocolate.) Review the day. Examine a still-painful negative from the day. Maybe someone said something that hurt or angered you and the hurt lingers on. Past hurts wound only if you keep the hurt alive, and yet letting go is not always easy. The bigger the hurt, the harder to let go, but you owe it to yourself to get free of past hurts. Take a minute to name the hurt. In the same way a feeling is better managed if named, so are the hurts of others toward us.

So think about the hurt and name it. Did the person treat you unfairly? Take without giving in return? Break a promise? Betray a hope? Embarrass you in public? Say or do something cruel?

Name the hurt. Now turn it into a bird. Make it any bird you wish it to be. As it has been eating at your heart, however, it may help to make it into a bird of prey—a hawk, a vulture. Feel the pain it is creating for you. Thank the pain.

Yes, thank the pain. Remember that from negatives come positives. Pain reminds us to keep our hands out of the fire. Pain reminds us to enjoy the good when it comes. And finally, pain reminds us to be careful about expecting more than life can deliver. As the poet Alice Walker noted, it is best to "live frugally on surprise." Life has many valleys and peaks. Expecting otherwise is unrealistic. If you expect to be happy all the time, you will be disappointed. But if you don't expect to be happy, when you are, it will be a bonus.

So pain hurts, but it also brings its gifts. Honor those gifts, and when you have finished, clap your hands together and tell the pain and the memory to fly away. Take a deep breath. Smile. Breathe in and out. The past is over.

You are here and you are safe. Let the pains of the past go. See the person who hurt you asking forgiveness. Forgive—if not completely, then as much as you can. Remember, we all do the best we can. We all fail. We all need forgiveness.

Exercise Ten: Be grateful for what you have been given; remember what is good in you, those you love, this world
Do this exercise before falling asleep. Recall the good moments of the day. If it was a day that held little good, it

is even more important to spend a minute focusing on a positive. Honor your strength, your ability to endure and to stay on the side of good, to keep caring and striving to do what is right. Remember what it is you have to be grateful for. Hold good thoughts in your heart as you drift off to sleep.

FITTING EMOTIONAL FITNESS INTO A BUSY LIFE

The program just described sounds like a lot, but it is less time-consuming than it seems at first glance. Every parent I've trained who has made a commitment to practicing these ten exercises found the time. Many find that they can take more than a minute on each exercise, but when time is precious, even a minute is enough to strengthen a core skill and keep yourself and your feelings on an even keel.

Need convincing? Meet Sally Skeptical. Her doctor sent her to me for an Emotional Fitness Training® course in stress management. Her blood pressure was climbing, but, as a single parent of three, who had a full-time job and was also going to graduate school, she laughed when her doctor suggested she ease off her hectic schedule. The super-quick program I created for her formed the foundation for all my fitness programs.

I taught her to center in one session. She clarified her mission statement in the second session, and we set up her program in the third session. She canceled the fourth session because she was practicing on her own and feeling confident the program was helping. She called a month later to tell me her blood pressure had dropped, she felt less stressed, her kids thought she was easier to live with, and she was referring a friend.

Here's how we squeezed an Emotional Fitness Training routine into Sally Skeptical's overscheduled life. First, we set up a tape recorder and attached it to a timer. The purpose was to replace her alarm clock with beautiful music. The tape she choose was a lovely piano concerto. Across from her bed I had her place a peaceful picture. When she first heard the tape, she centered and for one minute listened to the music with her eyes closed. Then she stretched and sat up and spent a few breaths looking at the picture and listening to the music. This exercise ended when she said, "Thank you," and went on with her day.

We had condensed her mission statement to one line: Care. Share. Dare. That one line was posted on her mirror. As she got dressed each morning, combed her hair, and put on her makeup, she looked at her mission statement and thought about how she was going to further it during the day in some small way. She then centered, and for the space of four breaths saw herself doing what she had determined to do. Usually, she thought about doing something she normally didn't dare do. Like what? Speak up in class. Speak up in a meeting. Speak back firmly to someone who was rude.

Next was waking her kids. Before waking them, I had her center, make a Soft Face, and spend three breaths watching them sleep. On her own, she decided to wake them to music. She also had each pick a beautiful object to focus on when they first opened their eyes. Her son rebelled. But later she told me he had put a picture of a soaring eagle right across from his bed.

After waking her children, she spent a few quiet minutes enjoying her morning coffee. She loved coffee and set the pot up every night so it would be brewed when she awoke. She learned to center and spend a minute concentrating on the pleasure this first cup of coffee gave her. Being in the moment for her coffee became something she did just for herself. She also used that time to observe her feelings.

She loved to write poetry but rarely had the time. She kept a pen and paper at the table, and when she was done with her coffee, she spent five minutes working on her newest poem. Two of her poems had won awards. One was her favorite. She had that framed and posted on a wall in the dining room. On the days the words did not flow, she centered and read the framed poem.

She drove to work, and I had her find five things of natural beauty she could appreciate on her way to and from work each day. As driving often provides opportunity to exercise kindness, I asked her when she was most likely to get a little impatient and annoyed on her way to work. Every day traffic slowed to a crawl at a toll gate. Drivers jockeyed and bullied in efforts to get to the toll first. This daily pileup set her on edge. She accepted my suggestion that this would be a useful place to practice letting go of negatives and gratitude as well. She resented letting cars pull in front of her, but she learned to smile and graciously usher one or two in front of her. She dared to hold the line with any obvious traffic bully. When a particularly stressed driver was overly pushy, and she didn't dare to hold the line; she practiced letting go of her negative feelings. Then she thought about people who had nourished her.

When she first reached her desk, she spent five minutes and only five minutes doing something concrete to bring order to her day. Usually, she filed her phone messages from the day before. Then I had her list six things on her memo pad she knew she was going to get accomplished that day. These were never to be the big things she wanted to accomplish, and that is part of the process. A list might read:

Open mail.

Have lunch with Jane.

Call accounting and schedule meeting.

Compliment Harry on brochure.

Make appointment with Joe for job review.

Have herbal tea in the afternoon.

At the end of the day, she crossed every item off her list. Whatever else the day had held, she could see at the end of the day some things she had accomplished.

When we first set up this program she was amazed to discover she could practice it almost entirely before her morning coffee break.

"Seems too easy," she told me.

I agreed, but urged her to try it just the same. She did and it helped. Just because something is easy, doesn't mean it isn't effective. Walking is a popular physical fitness exercise because it is so easy. So try my program. Here's an easy way to get into the groove.

1. Add awareness to all the exercises you currently do by centering and doing them with conscious awareness.

2. One by one, a week at a time, add to your day the exercises you don't do.

Can't stand the thought of adding one "must do" thing to your daily schedule? OK. Here are some other things you can try. These are emotional fitness exercises that don't need to be practiced every day.

1. Add a renewal rite to your daily routine. A rite is any customary practice used for religious or other purposes. Customary means regularly occurring. Think back over your childhood. Review your family rituals. The pleasant ones are renewal rites. I've told you about a number of my mother's rites. Watching the sunset was one. Getting the children up during the night of the first snowfall for a walk was another. The special way our family had of celebrating birthdays and other holidays was part of our renewal rites. Renewal

rites can be brief or more drawn out. Most families have some renewal rites, whether it's going to church or a Shabbat dinner.

2. Plan family fun. When we were foster parents, Thursday night was movie night. Everyone had to go. No X-rated films. One week David and I decided what we would see, the next week the kids would vote. If it was someone's birthday week, they got to pick the movie. If being tied to a weekly outing would be burdensome, then make it monthly. Designate the third Saturday of every month "fun day."

3. Plan some regular just-for-you rites. Once a month, I meet a special friend for lunch or dinner. When the kids were younger, some friends and I formed a monthly night-out-for-mothers group.

4. Create small sanctuaries in your home and at your workplace. Create one you can see as you get up each morning and go to bed each night. If you are a two-job parent and go to work outside the home every day, create a sanctuary at work as well. A picture of someone you love can be a small sanctuary. I have pictures, sea glass, seashells, and rocks scattered about my office. The key is to use these sanctuaries as conscious sanctuaries. That means centering and focusing on the memory of love or the peace the sanctuary offers. I can

see my kids' pictures a hundred times a day.
When I take a deep breath, make a Soft Face,
and really see the picture, or the seashell, I am
doing an emotional fitness exercise.

5. Make a list of five things you do incredibly
   well. Look for small things: do you always remember other people's birthdays with a card?
   Make a great pot pie or fantastic cookies?
   These are the kinds of things we often do automatically and don't remember to honor.
   Post the list in one of your sanctuaries. Read
   the list daily. Congratulate yourself for what
   you do well.

6. Make a list of five things your children and
   the other important people in your life do
   well. Post that list where you and they can see
   it. Update the list.

7. Write a poem about someone you no longer
   see, but whom you remember as helping you
   be all you could be. Keep the poem where you
   can see it and read it every day. After you
   have read it, remember the person who nourished you.

8. Pass along the next compliment you hear
   about another person. If your best friend says
   something nice about her son, the next time
   you see the son, tell him what his mother
   said.

9. On the last day of the month, call a friend you haven't spoken to in a year or write a letter to a friend you speak to regularly. Tell them how important they are to you.

10. Every day before getting into bed, hug yourself. Just throw your arms straight out, and then wrap them around your shoulders as you tell yourself you're worthy of many hugs.

The more you can practice one or more of these exercises, the more your emotional fitness will grow. Each exercise helps you stay connected to what is enduring. The more we savor the good, enjoy the beauty of this world, stay attached to the spirit of caring that binds us all—the spirit of love—the more our emotional fitness grows and the better the world becomes for us and our children.

SUGGESTED READING LIST

The books listed below were particularly helpful to me in a number of ways. Some helped me understand feelings, others taught me some of the skills I've tried to teach you. This is a short list. It includes all the books I referred to, but some of these are scholarly, and may not interest everyone.

David Burns. *Feeling Good. The New Mood Therapy.* (New York: William Morrow, 1980). A useful self-help book that explores how errors in thinking lead to negative feelings. Borderline between an easy read and more scholarly works.

Robert Coles. *Children of Crisis: A Study of Courage and Fear.* (Boston: Little, Brown, 1967).

———. *The Political Life of Children.* (Boston: Atlantic Monthly Press, 1986).

———. *The Spiritual Life of Children.* (Boston: Houghton Mifflin, 1990).

———. *The Call of Service: A Witness to Idealism.* (Boston: Houghton Mifflin, 1993).

Stephen J. Covey. *The Seven Habits of Highly Effective People.* (New York: Simon & Schuster, 1989). This best-selling book introduced me to the concept of mission statements. I particularly like the emphasis on balanced living and integrity.

Albert Ellis and Robert Harper. *A New Guide to Rational Living.* (New York: Institute for Rational-Emotive Therapy, 1973). Not as easy to read as some, but considered by many to be the big book when it comes to examining the beliefs underlying our beliefs.

Adele Farber and Elaine Mazlish. *Siblings Without Rivalry*. (New York: Avon Books, 1988). The only way to have siblings without rivalry is not to have a second child. Still, this is a very useful book for spelling out the tangled feelings siblings need to learn to manage.

Victor Frankel. *Man's Search for Meaning*. (New York: Simon & Schuster, 1984). Spells out the importance of having a life-affirming philosophy.

Robert Fulghum. *All I Really Need To Know I Learned In Kindergarten*. (New York: Random House, 1988). If everyone remembered these lessons and followed them there would be peace in our time.

James Garbarino. *Raising Children in a Socially Toxic Environment*. (San Francisco: Jossy Bass, 1995). Garbarino is the expert on trauma and children. He underscores the importance of taking care of parents, so the parents can take care of the kids.

Haim G. Ginnot. *Between Parent and Child*. (New York: Avon Books, 1976). One of the first books to stress the importance of communicating. Also one of the few how-to-talk-to-kids books that didn't leave me feeling guilty.

Daniel Goleman. *Emotional Intelligence*. (New York: Bantam Books, 1995). Another best-selling book. Useful for explaining all the ways feelings affect well-being. Well researched, some good practical suggestions, but more theory than how-to.

Thomas Gordon. *Parent Effectiveness Training*. (New York: Peter H. Wyden, 1970). Following in Ginnot's footsteps, Gordon set out to improve the way parents talk to kids. Unfortunately, he went too far. He pushed the communication envelope and tried to teach parents to speak like therapists. Not always helpful. Less helpful was the idea that if the parent did as he said, parenting could be conflict free. Parenting cannot be conflict free and children need parents who speak like loving parents, not neutral therapists. At the same time, this book really does help when it comes to letting go of trying to control adolescents and maintaining a reasonable relationship as you do so.

Thich Nah Hanh. *Peace Is Every Step*. (New York: Bantam Books, 1992). Useful on two counts—learning to meditate and developing a life-affirming philosophy.

Jerome Kagan. *The Nature of the Child.* (New York: Basic Books, 1984). As I've noted in the book, Jerome Kagan has been one of my gurus when it comes to understanding feelings, particularly the importance of uncertainty in creating certain feelings.

Jerome Kagan and Sharon Lamb. *The Emergence of Morality in Young Children.* (Chicago: The University of Chicago Press, 1987). A very scholarly book. Useful in helping me understand the universality of certain moral principles.

Mark Katz. *On Playing A Poor Hand Well.* (New York: W. W. Norton, 1996). School problems create negative emotions in children and in parents. This book tells both professionals and parents the ins and outs of surviving learning disabilities without undue damage to self-esteem or emotional fitness. The tactics are useful for dealing with any major life problem.

George Kelly. *A Theory of Personal Constructs.* (New York: W. W. Norton, 1952). Not a book for light reading. Included because I quoted from it.

Lawrence LaShan. *How to Meditate.* (New York: Bantam Books, 1984). This remains the classic meditation book. Well written. Easy to understand.

Katherine Levine. *When Good Kids Do Bad Things.* (New York: Pocketbooks, 1992). My first book. Interesting for those who want to see why I decided that learning to manage my negative feelings was so important.

Marsha M. Linehan. *Skills Training Manual for Treating Borderline Personality Disorder.* (New York: Guilford Press, 1993). Intended for therapists, but contains lots of useful self-help information.

Adolph Moser. *Don't Pop Your Cork on Monday.* (Kansas City: Landmark Editions, 1990). A great book to read to children as it helps explain to them that everyone has feelings, even parents, and that feelings can be managed.

Carol Tavris. *Anger: The Misunderstood Emotion.* (New York: Simon & Schuster, 1982). Everything you ever wanted to know about anger and a little bit more.

To learn more about Emotional Fitness Training® courses, workshops, Pocket Coach® kits, and other Emotional Fitness self-help materials, call toll-free 888-434-3424.